ADVICE FROM THE
SOCCER
PROS

To Gio,

All the best for becoming the best soccer player you can be. The soccer pros in this book can tell you how.

Always play your best,

Dave Farie

12-19-2011

ADVICE FROM THE SOCCER PROS

David Faries

ANDERSON WORLD, INC.

Library of Congress Cataloging in Publication Data

Faries, David, 1938 -
  Advice from the soccer pros.

  1. Soccer—Addresses, essays, lectures. I. Title.
GV943.F37   796.334'2   79-64730
ISBN: 0-89037-219-5

PHOTO CREDITS

Harrison Funk—10, 36, 57, 67, 95, 103; A. M. Rapping—85, 152; Bill Smith—18; Fred Anderson—48; Ken Reimer, 121; John Paul Ruplenas—133; George Coates—147; Michael Jacobs—161; and the following professional soccer teams: San Jose Earthquakes, Houston Hurricane, Ft. Lauderdale Strikers, and the San Diego Sockers.

Cover Photograph by Julian Baum

Anderson World, Inc.
Mountain View, California

Advice From the Soccer Pros is dedicated to all the players in the North American Soccer League who give their time and share their skills, knowledge, and love of the game with youth soccer players everywhere.

Contents

Foreword

Advice From The Soccer Pros tells how nineteen of the best players in the North American Soccer League play the game. Advice is given on developing skills and improving technique, tactics, and game strategy.

In the Forwards section, top goal scorers give tips on shooting, passing, beating a defender, scoring from inside and outside the box, off-the-ball movement, heading, dribbling, fakes and feints, crosses, and corner kicks.

The Midfielders section includes playmaking, controlling the game, offensive and defensive roles, teamwork, styles of play, throw-ins, free kicks, passing, and other skills.

In the Defenders section, advice is given on organizing the defense, channeling and tackling, defensive tactics and strategy, reading the game, positioning, counterattacks, and overlapping. The Goalkeepers section includes arcs and how to narrow the angle, diving, positioning for crosses and corner kicks, concentration, and working with the defenders.

Special attention is given to mental preparation and attitude, and how professional soccer players have used their imaginations to improve their game and individual talents.

Everything in the book is geared to improvement and bringing out the best in every player.

Acknowledgments

This book would not have been possible without the help of my wife Vivien.

Special thanks is also given to Pepe Pinton and Raul Alvernaz.

Thanks is also given for the fine work of photographers Harrison Funk, Rick Martin, and Anacleto Michael Rapping.

Since some players may change clubs after the book goes to press, team affiliations given here may not be correct.

Part One

The Forwards

Paul Child
Memphis Rogues

Alertness is a big part of center forward Paul Child's game. Because he is always aware of everything going on around him in the penalty area, he can take advantage of the split-second scoring opportunities by being in the right position to receive passes from his teammates or to capitalize on a defensive mistake.

This knack for reading the game has earned Child the position of third All-Time leading scorer in the NASL with 77 goals and 36 assists in his eight years with the league. Before joining the Memphis Rogues in 1980, Child was a founding member of the San Jose Earthquakes and possessed almost all of the club's major scoring records.

"If one of my teammates takes a quick shot on goal from say twenty-five yards out, I'm going to follow it in," Child explained. "As soon as you see your teammate about to take the shot, turn and sprint toward the goalkeeper. In one out of ten times, the ball will hit the goalkeeper in the chest and bounce on the ground, or maybe the ball will hit his hand and fall to the ground. There is your chance of getting a garbage goal. A goal is a goal. You don't really care what kind of a goal it is because every goal counts."

Child has also scored goals when the ball has struck the goalpost and bounced out. The goalkeeper often dives for the ball, and lands on the ground, unable to recover.

"If you're in position to get a foot on the ball, all you have to do is push it into the net," Child said. "It's really all just being alert and watching for other people to make mistakes."

Child also is ready for when a defender makes a mistake with the ball and tries to hustle him into making an error. If a defender dribbles the ball five or ten yards away from you and stops, he may figure you are too far away to tackle him. Keep a casual look on your face and do not show any sign that you plan to go after the ball. He may even look away from you to see where he can pass the ball. The instant he looks away, go after the ball. You should travel those five or ten yards within 2 seconds. When the goalkeeper sees you coming, he may be startled and lose control of the ball. His mistake gives you an opportunity to tackle the ball away and score.

Hustling an opponent into making an error does not mean running into him to give him a hard time in order to make him worry about you. Those tactics are to be avoided. Be crafty.

When a forward makes a mistake, like losing the ball to a defender, you cannot allow yourself to become depressed. Instead of feeling sorry for yourself or trying to blame somebody else for your mistake, recover by making yourself more alert.

"Concentrate with everything in your mind to win that ball back. You gain a tremendous amount of mental effort doing that. Always be on the attack, every minute of the game," Child said.

Child has always been an aggressive player. Born in Birmingham, England on December 8, 1952, his parents bought him a soccer ball at age four. Since he lived near a soccer field, he and his friends played there every day, kicking the ball, playing games, learning how to do different things with the ball. By his thirteenth birthday, scouts from Aston Villa, a first division soccer club, spotted him and signed an option with him to play on a junior team sponsored by the professional team. Coached by professionals, Child and the other players were groomed for the professional ranks.

Although Child concentrates before the game while he gets dressed in the locker room, he is still confronted by a

Paul Child (10)

certain amount of tension. "When I go down the ramp to the field, I'm very nervous until the whistle blows to start the game. Then I just start releasing those tensions when I start running. I run until I've let out my steam," he said. "The more I run, the faster the tension and nervousness disappears. Then I settle down."

While running is a big part of his game, Child's style of running has changed from year to year. "The more experienced you get, the less running you'll do in a game," he noted. "In the past six years, I think I've slowed down a little bit. I make the ball do the work now, whereas before I was just running. Each year my game improves with experience. The more experience you have, the better you read the game and know what you want to do before you do it."

Physical fitness is an integral part of Child's training. Because he has the strength and stamina to play the last minute of a 90 minute game with the same enthusiasm and energy he did the first minute of the game, he never lets down and is always ready to take advantage of every scoring opportunity no matter how late in the game it comes.

Along with physical fitness, Child continuously works on improving his skills and techniques. "You can never learn too much about soccer," he said. "Every play is different. The more you practice and the more games you play, the more experience you'll gain, and the better player you will be."

Giorgio Chinaglia
New York Cosmos

No center forward in the North American Soccer League has acquired more fame and goals in the last four years than All-Star Giorgio Chinaglia. Among his honors and achievements as striker for the famed New York Cosmos is his standing as the top all-time scorer in the League. He averages 1 goal for every 2 shots. In 1978 and 1979 the naturalized citizen from Italy was named to the NASL All-Star first team.

Because his 6-foot height gives him a long-legged stride, Chinaglia can beat defenders to a ball passed to the open space in front of him. The more room he has to maneuver around in the penalty box area, the better his chances to score.

He relies on his instincts to create scoring opportunities, often capitalizing on mistakes by defenders marking him. "Soccer is not a game where you can dictate moves like set plays," he explained. "The only set plays you have are free kicks. As far as forwards, you use your instincts."

Born in Carrera, Italy, Chinaglia immigrated with his family to Wales in Great Britain where his parents operated a restaurant. Like many European boys, he started playing with a soccer ball at an age too young to remember. "I played from morning until night when I was a kid," he recalled. "At school we had the soccer team, then we'd come out of school and go to the park and everybody would play."

He spent a lot of time kicking a ball against the wall. The hours he devoted to shooting and trapping the ball helped him develop his ball control, heading, passing, and shooting skills. Not satisfied just to play one game on Saturday with his school team, he also played on a youth league team which played a game every Sunday. Since he did not receive any formal coaching until he was a teenager, he acquired his skills from playing with older, more experienced youth players, watching games, and experimenting with different techniques.

At age 15 he played center forward for a Welsh professional soccer club. His talents and skills were so developed by then that he bypassed apprenticeship on the reserve team and became a starter on the first team.

He returned to Italy at age 19 and played the 1966-67 season with Massesse in Division C. Then he transferred to Internapoli, also in Division C, where he played two years. In 1969 his contract was purchased in Lazio of Rome in Division B. Chinaglia took it upon himself to build Lazio into a top team, capable of successfully competing in the first division.

Through his leadership and goal scoring abilities, he instilled a new spirit of self-confidence and teamwork in the team which carried them into Division A.

Compared to the NASL, Italian soccer matches and European games in general, usually end with lower scores. Chinaglia's record of 98 goals in the 209 games he played for Lazio from 1969 to 1976 is excellent. Chinaglia's average of a goal almost every other game made him the top scorer for Lazio as he led the club to the Italian League Championship in 1973 and 1974 and won the scoring title.

Chinaglia was the only second-division player on the Italian National Team playing against West Germany in the 1974 World Cup final.

He and his American-born wife and family moved to the United States in 1976 when the Cosmos purchased his contract from Lazio. He was successful his first season in New York, scoring 19 goals with 11 assists.

Chinaglia is a hard worker, dedicated player, and loves to score goals. "You must score goals to win games," Chinaglia said. "Always give 100 percent of yourself. There are times when you're going to play bad, but always give 100 percent. You have to contribute in some way to the team. That is a must for every player."

In today's game, center forwards do not have time to try fancy moves in the penalty area. Every move requires split-second timing. "If you have good timing, you meet the ball, connect with it easier, and the ball will go into the net faster," Chinaglia said.

Chinaglia's victory celebration is a sharing of his scoring triumph with his teammates and the fans. "I want to give the fans what they paid to come and see, the ball roll into the back of the net," he said. "I get a great satisfaction in scoring goals. I love scoring goals. It gives me a great feeling to help the team win and give pleasure to the fans."

The scoring of a goal in soccer may have more emotional attachment for the scorer, his teammates, and the fans than in any other sport. The emotional pressures that build with the hope, fears, and expenditures of energy and frustration may very well be unequalled in all other sports.

Every goal he scores gives Chinaglia happy satisfaction, regardless of whether he scores in practice or a league game. "All goals are goals, and I celebrate all of them," he said. Of course, a game-winning goal and a tie-breaking goal does carry special significance to him.

Regardless whether the team is behind or ahead, Chinaglia's concentration on scoring is consistent. If the team is behind and he has missed every attempt, he does not permit any depression to set in.

"Don't look for a goal. Then it will come automatically," he advised. "I went through a period in 1977 in 7 games where my shots were hitting the crossbar and the posts. I hit the goalposts 20 times that year. Even though you want to score more than anything else, you must not think about it. Just hope your luck will change and then let it happen. Once you break the ice, everything will be normal and you will start scoring again."

The more successful Chinaglia is, the more difficult the opponent teams try to make it for him to score. Some teams

Giorgio Chinaglia (9)

will assign two defenders to mark him and occasionally have a third defender close by in support.

"You musn't think about the defender. Concentrate on your own moves and the way you're going to play," Chinaglia explained. "The defender is going to be there anyway so it's useless to worry about him. Control the ball and try to get it in the back of the net."

A defender may mark Chinaglia so tightly that he may never touch a ball in 85 minutes of play. Then in the eighty-seventh minute, the defender may make that one mistake and Chinaglia scores.

"I am always looking for opportunities," he said. "You must concentrate on scoring the entire 90 minutes of every game."

Before a game starts, he thinks about how he wants to play, pondering different ways he may be able to create scoring opportunities for himself and his teammates. During the first 10 minutes of a match, he focuses his attention on getting into the game. "No matter how much pregame warm-up you do, you still need to loosen up when the game starts," Chinaglia explained. "In the first two or three minutes, you seldom see anybody sprint 30 to 40 yards. Try to touch the ball and pass it around. Get a feel for the game."

Chinaglia's style of play as a center forward calls for playing most of the game in the penalty area, looking for the cross from the wing and pass from the midfield, always ready to capitalize on a defender's mistake.

"The most important thing is to get married to the penalty area," he said. "You must know every inch of it. You must be boss of the penalty area, and you must know what you want to do when the ball comes to you."

When you're in the 6-yard box and a fullback marks you tight, drift out right or left toward the 18-yard line. If the defender does not follow you, you will be free when the ball comes into the area. If the defender moves back with you, take him out as far as the 18-yard line. If he still stays with you, remain out there to see if he continues to mark you or if he starts watching the ball and forgets you. When the ball comes into the penalty area, you are free to sprint to it and take a shot on goal, Chinaglia explained.

If the defender continues marking you tight on the 18-yard line and your winger brings the ball down the side, Chinaglia said, do not rush back into the goalmouth. If you do then the defender will just stay with you and try to block any attempt you make to get the ball. The defender may shift his concentration to the ball and lose track of you, or he may even rush back toward the goalmouth to protect his zone. Should that happen, you are again free.

According to Chinaglia, in the situation where the defender still marks you tight, then move away from the ball or toward the opposite side of the penalty area. Try to get out of his line of vision. If the defender starts concentrating on watching the ball instead of you, you may find yourself unmarked.

"That's a mistake defenders will sometimes make, just

looking at the ball all the time," Chinaglia said. "So that's when you capitalize on their mistakes."

Chinaglia prefers to have the ball played into an open space in front of him instead of at his feet. With his long stride, he can outsprint a defender and run onto the ball, and try to take a shot on goal or pass to a teammate who can take a shot.

If a ball is played to your feet and you have to dribble and beat at least one defender before taking a shot, the risks of losing the ball are greater than when the ball is passed into an open space in front of you.

Less experienced forwards should take a quick look at the goalkeeper and the goal before striking the ball. "After you have gained sufficient experience and confidence, you will be able to hit the ball into the back of the net without looking," Chinaglia said.

In his youth soccer camps, which he conducts during the summertime, Chinaglia teaches you how to get power behind your shot. Approach the ball in a gentle manner. "It's the swinging movement and the balance of the body that give the leg the most powerful shot," he explained. "Many players kick the ball from the body. Use the whole body, swinging your leg to get your most powerful shot."

Know where you want to place your shot, Chinaglia said. Unless you concentrate on where you want your shot to go, your shot may go wild or right to the goalkeeper. During practice sessions when you take shots on goal, tell yourself where you want the ball to go, the right or left side, upper or bottom corner.

Whether you stike the ball with the instep, inside or outside of the foot depends on how the ball comes to you. Until a player has mastered all three kicks, his scoring ability will be limited. You should also be able to shoot with either foot. Then you will not have to unbalance yourself in always trying to hit the ball with only your right foot or only your left foot.

"A bouncing ball or a ball coming toward you are the best. You can run onto it and hit with a lot of power,"

Chinaglia said. "If the ball is going away from you, you cannot put as much power behind it."

Chinaglia sometimes will try scoring on the near post with a banana shot, even though the goalkeeper is right in front of him. If he can curl the ball around the goalkeeper, almost nothing can prevent the ball from going into the back of the net.

When you are tightly marked and the ball is played to you, pass the ball back to a teammate. If the defender marking you moves to your right and creates an open space on your left, your teammate can pass the ball into the open space for you to run onto. Practice this move with a passer and a defender.

If this succeeds, and the fullback goes for the ball on your left side, he has probably opened up a space on your right. One of your midfielders may run past you into the open space and have an opportunity to score. Pass him the ball before a defender can try to tackle him or block his shot.

Chinaglia plays a lot of 1-2's, also known as wall passes, in the penalty area, which is one reason why he has made more than 35 assists since joining the Cosmos.

A successful 1-2 pass requires quickness and teamwork, especially in the 6-yard box area. Work on wall passes with your teammates until you can do them well. Then add a defender so you learn to receive and pass the ball under pressure.

Get to know your teammates, their individual styles of play, and capabilities. If a teammate has excellent passing technique and usually positions himself well to receive and pass accurately in wall-pass situations in the penalty area, practice together and learn his preferences in having the ball passed to him. He will learn just how far to lead the ball in front of you on the return pass for you to take your best shot on goal.

The more you practice crosses, corner kicks, free kicks, and passes with your teammates, the better your timing will be. Good timing is essential in scoring goals, according to Chinaglia.

Timing is also important in off-the-ball movement. "If

you can create space for a teammate to run into and shoot the ball into the back of the net, then you're playing well," he said. "If all the defenders and forwards are in the penalty area, then it's impossible to score unless you get lucky. If you're marked tight and can't get the ball, draw away as many opponents as you can." The more space you create for your teammate, the better his chances for scoring.

To become a good center forward, you really have to train hard. "I usually do everything my teammates do in practice, but at the end of the training session, I stay out with the goalkeeper," Chinaglia said. "I take five or six balls and I shoot at the goal from all different angles. I go all around the 18-yard box, play with the ball a little bit, and then boom, straight away shoot on goal. Try to shoot from everywhere around the box."

Good health is extremely important for a soccer player, Chinaglia said. Eat the right foods, stay away from drugs and alcohol. Train and develop your body to do everything you want in a game. Always strive to improve your skills and techniques to the highest level you can achieve.

"My own philosophy is I have to go out and play the best I can all the time, no matter what happens," he emphasized. "Always give 100 percent for the team."

Karl-Heinz Granitza
Chicago Sting

Renowned for his powerful and accurate left-footed shot, Karl-Heinz Granitza is a dangerous scoring threat from either side of the penalty area. With twenty goals and ten assists, he tied for sixth place among the top scorers in the NASL in 1979 and led the Chicago Sting to the playoffs.

Granitza always has concentrated on being the best soccer player he possibly can. The son of a miner, he was born in Lunan, a city in central West Germany, on November 1, He played very little soccer until age nine when he received his first soccer ball and shoes.

"I slept with my soccer ball," he recalled. "My dream from then on was to become a professional soccer player."

Karl-Heinz learned the basics from his father who played amateur soccer. "My father said, 'If you want to play soccer, work first in school and afterwards you can play soccer. Play whatever you like. If you like soccer more than anything else, then play it all the time.'"

Like most professionals Granitza played soccer every minute he was not in school. Since his family lived in a large apartment complex, there were lots of older and younger boys to play with. He usually played with the older boys because they taught him techniques and challenged him to play on their level.

Since Lunan did not have a professional soccer team, all the youth teams were organized under the amateur soccer

club, which was founded about 1908. Granitza joined his
first team at age ten. "It was a very good youth club," he
said. "I was taught so much by my coach, Werner Klaosa,
who is still my friend after all these years."

Klaosa coached him until he reached fifteen. Granitza's
father also worked with him the first three or four years.
"When the kids from the apartment building had no time
to play, he came out and we kicked the ball around. It was
always fun."

Although he has become one of the top goal scorers in the
NASL and the West German Bundesliga, Granitza did not
play center forward until he was 22. From the time he started
playing soccer at age ten until he reached 15, he played
sweeper and defender.

At age 15 he played midfielder for the Dortmund amateur
club. During the next three years he played with Dortmund,
the club won four titles. Because scouts and coaches from the
Bundesliga rarely came out to look for top quality players
in the small communities like the one where Granitza lived,
his talents went unrecognized by any of the first division
clubs. At age 18 he signed with Lunan which was now a
second division club. His dream was still to play in the
Bundesliga.

After playing three years for Lunan, Karl-Heinz went to
Gutersloh also in the second division. While he started out
a left fullback at Lunan, the coach moved him to the midfield. "I played defensive midfielder, that was my favorite
position at that time," Granitza said. "But when you play
defense in the middle third (of the field) you run so much
but you do not score many goals. I have no chance for the
first division. You only have a chance when you're scoring
goals and the coaches from the first division come to see
you play."

Karl-Heinz finally got his chance after he joined Rochling,
another second division team, in 1974. The coach of Rochling
pulled the center forward, who was having a very bad season,
and replaced him with Granitza. During the six months
remaining in the season and the following year, he scored
25 goals.

"Playing center forward is very different from playing defensive midfield and defender," Granitza said. "Your concentration is different. The center forward must find chances for scoring goals. You always concentrate 100 percent on scoring goals.

Granitza taught himself how to play the center forward position. He went to every Bundesliga game he could and watched how the center forwards played. He watched how they controlled the ball, dribbled and faked defenders, positioned themselves in front of the goal, worked with the wingers and midfielders, attacked goalkeepers and defenders one-on-one, and how they headed and shot goals. He took in every detail and went home and practiced what he had seen until he perfected it himself.

"The first thing you learn is shooting technique," Granitza explained. "You practice shooting every day, shooting with the left foot, the right foot, scoring with head balls. You must practice different things every day, pass the ball, stop the ball, hold the ball, control it, shoot it. When I played midfield I practiced passing the ball to the free man, now as a forward I had to learn to make opportunities to score goals."

Practice and play until you play by instinct. When you rely on your instinct, you forget about thinking about the game and analyzing how you are playing, Granitza said. Instinct allows you to flow with the game, everything you do comes automatically from your skills and experience.

"Your mind is relaxed," he said. "If you are 100 percent concentration, you're not thinking, your instinct comes through. Your concentration allows you to play by instinct."

At age 23, he transferred to Rochling in the second division, where he scored 29 goals that season. That scoring record attracted the attention of coaches and scouts from the Bundesliga. Hertha Berlin offered him a contract and the next season found him playing for one of the top clubs in the West German first division. Granitza's dream had come true.

He played center forward for Hertha Berlin from 1976 through the 1978 season, coming on loan to the Sting in the summer of 1978. After scoring 19 goals with nine assists in 22 games for Chicago, the owners bought his contract from Hertha and signed Granitza to a five-year contract here.

Karl-Heinz Granitza (12)

In addition to his ability to score with power shots 16 to 25 yards out from the goal, he can also curl the ball around a corner of the goal from the same distances.

"I make a lot of curl shots during practices from around the 18-yard line, some in the right corner and some in the left," he said. "While my best banana shot is with the inside of the foot, you must find out what is the best way for you to kick a boomerang ball," Granitza said.

Banana balls, boomerangs, and curls are all names for shots that bend in or out (like a banana or C-shape). Practi . kicking the ball with the inside of the foot to make the ball curl inside. If you bend the ball with the outside of the foot, the ball will curve to the outside.

"If you have the ball, a defender is running out trying to block your shot and the goalkeeper is on his near post, stop the ball if you have time and try to bend it around the defender into the long corner," Granitza explained. "If you keep the ball on the ground, the goalkeeper has little chance of preventing it from going into the far corner. If you kick the ball high, the goalkeeper might be able to save it."

Sometimes when the ball is passed to you, the goalkeeper and defenders will run to the near post, giving you the opportunity to stop the ball and place the shot. Take advantage of the time and aim your shot into the far post. If a defender is marking you tight and you cannot take time to look at the goal and see where the opponents are positioned, shoot by instinct.

Often, the center forward will approach the goal with the ball from the side or at an angle instead of being right in front of the goalmouth. To get yourself in proper position to shoot, turn your body slightly toward the goal, and plant your non-kicking foot with your toes pointed at the goal. When you kick the ball, it will go in the direction your toes are pointed, Granitza said.

If you are running toward the goal at an angle and the ball is passed to you from behind, control the ball, slow it down, with the outside of the foot. Take another step and turn and shoot with the same technique described above. The more you practice taking shots on goal from different angles, the better you will be able to score goals in games.

When the ball is crossed in the air to the center forward in front of the goal, but not high enough to head it, hit the ball on the volley before it touches the ground.

"If you wait until the ball gets on the ground, a defender may tackle you to try to block your shot. Hit the ball on the volley with your instep into the back of the net," Granitza said. "You see the ball and then it's 100 percent instinct. Most of the time you do not have time to look at the goalkeeper and the goal. You just shoot."

If the ball comes in from the left side, strike it with your left foot. If the ball is crossed from the right side, hit it with your right foot. "But if you have no chance with the right foot, use your left foot," he said. "Use whichever foot is in position, but try to get your timing so you hit it with the correct foot."

Strike the ball with your instep rather than the inside of your foot because the instep gives you more power. You want a lot of power because that makes the shot harder for the goalkeeper to save. Also keep your shot low for the same reason.

When the winger speed dribbles down the wing and you sprint down the center of the field toward the goal, keep your eye on the winger and maintain his pace. At the same time you are running to the goal, turn your upper body a little sideways toward the winger. When he crosses the ball, your body is in a better position for you to take a shot on goal. This is a basic tactic in soccer offense.

"Be sure to keep your body between the ball and the stopper. If you let the defender get ballside of you, you have almost no chance of getting a shot on goal," Granitza said.

Contrary to other strikers like Giorgio Chinaglia, when the ball is passed on the ground to Granitza, he prefers the ball played to his feet rather than to an open space a yard or two in front of him. "I do not want the ball played into free room in front of me because the stopper and the sweeper are also trying to get the ball. You have little chance against two opponents. The sweeper thanks you for the ball and clears it," he explained. "It's very important for the winger to play the ball to your feet."

When you take a shot, Granitza said, bend your body over the ball. If you are shooting with your right foot, plant your left foot beside the ball. When you go to strike the ball, bring your right knee over the ball, and hit it with power.

"To hit the ball with power, you need good leg muscles," he said. "If you have weak muscles, then you must exercise every day and use weights." Under the guidance of his soccer coach Granitza exercised and used weights three times a week to develop his leg muscles when he was about 15 to 18 years old.

"When you have little muscle, you have no chance of becoming a good soccer player," he said. "The most important thing for a soccer player is technique, after this, you must have good muscles. But it's not good if you develop your muscles too much." Bulky muscles will reduce your speed and agility. He worked with weights to strengthen his arms and shoulders, as well as his whole body.

Granitza's style of play in the NASL is a little different than when he played in the West German Bundesliga. Here he receives mostly passes to his feet with some long balls. The long ball was rarely ever used when he played center forward for Hertha Berlin. He uses his quickness to turn with the ball on the defender and take a shot on goal. While he can shoot with either foot, he prefers to use his left.

Most of Granitza's goals are scored in the area from the 18- to the 6-yard line. With his shooting ability, he can score from almost anywhere inside or outside the penalty box.

When you have your back to the goal and the ball is passed to your feet, be ready to turn to the right or left. Spread your arms out and back a little bit. If the defender marks you tight, you can feel where he is. If he is on your right side, turn left and shoot. If he is on your left, turn the ball on your right side and take a shot. Always turn and shoot in the same movement. Any hesitation gives the defender time to try to tackle the ball away from you or block your shot, Granitza explained.

If the defender bumps you before you turn and makes it difficult for you to control the ball, pass it back to your midfielder. If he is not in a position to take a shot on goal, he can pass the ball to someone who is. He could also pass the ball into an open space beside or behind you, giving you an opportunity to turn and shoot. The midfielder might also pass it out to the wing who could cross it back into the center for you to head or shoot into the back of the net.

When you have your back to the goal and a defender marks you tight before you get the pass, you can run forward a yard or two toward the ball being passed to you, control and turn the ball all in one movement, and take the defender on one-on-one.

Granitza loves to score goals. "I want to win every game," he said. "From the beginning when I started playing, I wanted goals. To become a good forward, you have to want to score goals and move direct to the goal. You have to play by instinct."

The years he played fullback, sweeper, and defensive midfielder give him an advantage over his opponents because he understands how to play their positions, their individual and team tactics, so he can think like a defender when he wants to figure how they will play against him.

"It is good for center forwards to take defense positions in practice games, especially early in the week. You learn to tackle, mark a man, defensive heading, all the techniques a defender uses in the game. This helps you know how a defender thinks and it will help you beat the defender marking you in a game," Granitza explained. "Then later in the week, play center forward and test out the things you learned in the first part of the week. This will help improve your instincts."

Although Granitza has become a top star in the NASL and Bundesliga, he has not permitted fame and fortune to change him. "You cannot let it go to your head, you live the same life," he said. "No matter how great you are, you cannot eat nothing but caviar and drink only champagne. That is no good. It is very important that you are always the same person."

To become a quality player, Granitza said, you must work hard every day, learn the techniques, and develop your skill.

Kyle Rote, Jr.
Houston Hurricane

The first rookie and only native American to lead the NASL in scoring, Kyle Rote, Jr. piloted the Dallas Tornado to the league championship in 1973. With an average of one goal per game, he became the all time leading scorer for Dallas during his six seasons with the Tornado. In 1979, he was traded to the Houston Hurricane, involving the highest purchase price ever paid for an American soccer player. He is the only three-time winner of the ABC Superstar competition.

Rote has always worked hard at every sport he has played. Born in Dallas, Texas on December 25, 1950, he spent much of his childhood in New York where his father played football with the Giants. Young Rote was a natural athlete who excelled in football, basketball, and baseball.

Though his father was a famous football star, he always supported Kyle Jr. in everything he did except his involvement in athletics.

"He did not want me to feel any pressure because we were growing up in New York where he was a big football hero," Rote said. "He wanted to make sure no one could ever say to me, 'Kyle, you're good because your dad helped you.' So while he was interested in what I did athletically, he was just as interested in how I did in my music lessons and other things. He actually showed more interest in my school work than he did in my athletics, which is wonderful. So I

23

know I'm playing soccer not because of any pressure from him, but because I want to."

When Rote, Sr. retired from professional football in 1961, the family moved back to Dallas. In high school young Kyle lettered in football, basketball, and baseball. He did not kick a soccer ball until he was 16 years old. He and his friends on the football team only became interested in soccer because they wanted a fun physical activity to keep themselves in condition during the summertime before the fall high school football season started.

Since none of them knew anything about soccer and no coach was available, Rote and his friends studied the few available books on the sport and tried to teach themselves the basic skills and techniques of the game.

"The reason I think I enjoy soccer so much is because initially we got a team together and played without a coach. We practiced hard every day. We taught ourselves," he recalled. "It kept a lot of fun in what we were doing, so we looked forward every day to going out and practicing."

Rote believes many youth coaches today spend too much time on drills and tactics instead of letting kids enjoy the game. "The skills will come, if the kids are having fun. They'll want to learn," he noted. "The prime goal of the coach should be to develop an atmosphere where the kids can have fun and want to learn."

In the fall Rote returned to quarterbacking the football team at Highland Park High School. His football talent became so well known that he received offers for more than fifty college football scholarships before he graduated the following year. Oklahoma State University was his choice. He played freshman football until he suffered a broken femur and damaged ligaments during a football practice. After an operation and physical therapy, he was pronounced in even better condition than before the injury.

Because he did not find the kind of academic atmosphere he wanted at OSU, Rote transferred to the University of the South in Sewanee, Tennessee at the end of his freshman year.

Both soccer and football were played at the university

Kyle Rote, Jr. (12)

and because the seasons overlapped, he had to choose which sport he wanted to play.

And soccer won. He played three years of varsity soccer and was the team's most valuable player each year, as well as team captain in the last two years.

After graduation, Rote was drafted by the Dallas Tornado where he played six seasons. In 1979, the club sold Rote to the Houston Hurricane for the highest price ever paid for an American soccer player.

Because he has a great talent of scoring with his head, Rote plays most of the game in front of the goalmouth.

"I would rather head a ball when it's crossed than try to trap it, get it off the ground, and try to dribble past somebody for a shot," he said. "My style is to stay in the middle and use my size, speed, and jumping abilities to get into dangerous positions on either the near or far post for headers and shots. If I'm tightly marked, I will move around, taking two defenders, if I can, wherever I go, clearing a space for a midfielder to run into and head or shoot."

The path of the ball's flight is also a critical factor in determining where he will head the crossed ball. "There are times when the ball is crossed way over the back post at an angle that's almost impossible to shoot," Rote explained. "Instead, I'll play it back to a teammate who is in a better position. This means I have to know where everybody is. So when the ball is kicked, I'll take a quick look around to see where the other players are, just in case I have to lay it off."

Before the cross is taken he usually positions himself on the edge of the 18-yard box. When the ball is hit, he makes his run to the far post where he jumps up to head the ball. A running jump gives him far more heading power than jumping from a standing position. If two teammates have already positioned themselves at the far post, he will make his run to the near post.

If you run to the near post, run to a specific spot where you expect the ball to be driven, hit hard to you. If the ball is floated to the near post, you have more time to adjust your run to where you can head the ball, Rote said.

"In making your run, try to position yourself so the

defender marking you has to watch either the ball or you," he explained. "You also want to be where the goalkeeper can't watch both you and the ball. Try to stay a little wider than the defender. Then when the ball is hit and he looks at it, you can get in front of him before he has a chance to react. Always try to get goalside of the defender."

By staying wider than the defender marking you, you can watch both him and the ball. Do the same with the goalkeeper.

When you go up to head a ball crossed to the near post and the goalkeeper will also go up for the ball, head the ball to a teammate who is behind him. The teammate may have a perfect shot on goal and score from your pass. If the ball is driven hard to the near post, flick it over to a teammate at the far post. The goalkeeper is probably covering you, but may be unable to get across the goalmouth in time to block your teammate's head shot.

"In taking a head shot on goal, head the ball with power at the goal. If you have time, try and place it," Rote explained. "Try to hit low to the goal line because it is more difficult for a goalkeeper to dive out and down than it is straight out to the side and because it takes him more time. Sometimes we even try to bounce a header on the goal line so it will bounce back into the back of the net. If the goalkeeper does dive in time, he may mishandle the ball so it might roll out toward you, giving you another chance to score. If you can, head the ball to the side of the goal where the goalkeeper isn't. If you have time, aim it into one of the corners."

If you see that the goalkeeper expects you to head the ball with your forehead, you could head the ball with the side of your head, knocking it beside him. You can also fake the goalkeeper by looking at a corner before you head it, and then hitting the ball with the side of your head into the opposite side of the goal. With these "misdirect headers" you lose some power but you gain the advantage of the fake.

"If I'm making a run and I'm watching the near post, the goalkeeper realizes that by the way I'm running, I'll have to head it to the near post, if I want to get any power on the ball. So when he tries to cover that position, you've caught him going the wrong way and can flick the ball past him with the side of your head."

Timing your head shot is also very important. When the ball is crossed, make your run so you get in front of the defender, jump up, keep your eyes on the ball, and head it at the top of your jump. If you fail to get in front of the defender before you jump, he may be able to jump up and clear the ball away. You want to jump as high as you can because the goalkeeper can reach up with his hands when he challenges you for the ball. Therefore, you also want to position yourself between the goalkeeper and the ball, Rote explained.

"Assume that the maximum height you can jump and head the ball is seven-and-a-half feet," he said. "If the goalkeeper likes to catch balls close to his chest instead of outstretched hands, then you'll have that height advantage. Most of the time he will reach as far as he can for the ball, so you have to get up as high as you can in the air."

Always jump up before the defender does. If you can get up first, the momentum of his jump will help keep you in the air. You will also prevent him from using your back and shoulder as leverage to push himself higher in the air. If you jump up first, the referee can more easily observe any fouls the defender might try to commit.

"Use your stomach muscles as a source of power in heading, rather than your neck muscles. What you want to do is tighten your neck muscles and keep your head from wobbling when it hits the ball," Rote advised. "Your stomach muscles are among the strongest muscles in your body. The snap you can generate with your stomach muscles allows you a much longer arc than anything you could ever do with your neck muscles. If you move your neck forward and back you have an arc of maybe seven or eight inches. But with your stomach muscles you've got an arc of probably two feet. You can generate much more power in two feet than you can in seven inches.

"Always jump up even though you might not have to, because when you jump up, it gives you the ability to use your stomach muscles. Add that spring to your jump to head the ball instead of having to use your neck. By facing the ball, you won't lose power trying to rotate your head trying to hit it."

When a ball is chipped forward or driven hard in the air into the penalty area, it is difficult to head the ball into the goal. Unless you can touch the ball with your head and change its flight into the back of the net, pass it to a teammate, Rote said.

"Always try to pass the ball to your player's feet because it only takes one motion to trap and control the ball. If you pass it chest high, he has to trap it with his chest and then get it down to his feet. That extra motion can be costly," he said. "The easiest ball you can pass your teammate is to his feet."

If a ball is passed or crossed to you, and you are not in a position to shoot, you can skim head it back to a teammate behind you. When the ball comes to your head, bend your neck back, hit the ball with the top of your forehead, and let it bounce back and over your head to the player behind you.

Where you pass the ball is dictated by your teammates. "If a midfielder makes a good run, you can head the ball into a space you know he is going to run into."

Like the other soccer skills, heading requires lots of practice. "We do a lot of functional training," he said. "Take eight to ten balls and set them around the field. Then have someone hit them to you to head into the goal or pass back. Practice without opposition until you develop enough confidence that you're comfortable playing with a defender."

One drill he recommends calls for a winger to cross a ball into the middle for a forward to pass to a midfielder running toward the goal. Rather than trapping the ball, the midfielder should volley or shoot the second the ball touches the ground.

"If you and a friend are just out jogging, stay four to five yards apart, and pitch the ball to his head. He heads it back to you and you pitch again. Run backward so he has to head it while running forwards, then you run forward so he has to run backward and head it. Also do it running sideways," Rote suggested. "Get used to heading the ball from those different positions. It will help you in a game."

Rote believes you have to give 100 percent in every practice session. "Whether or not you're a natural athlete, you've got to work hard to develop yourself. You've got to have the self-discipline and the dedication to do it. You're the only one who can make that decision. Your success really depends on your own desire to achieve what you want to.

"By working hard in your teenage years to become a starting player on the soccer team, a top golfer, artist, or musician, you will realize later on in life that hard work is going to allow you to succeed in whatever else you do. You will have set the groundwork to do that kind of thing. You can say to yourself, 'I've pushed myself and sacrificed when I was younger, I can do it now.' That's the advantage I think competitive athletics gives young people. It allows them to test the ability of their bodies and push beyond what they think they can do."

Rote tries to improve himself every day. "It's not just in the area of athletics either. I think I'm a goal-oriented person. I have goals in my life whether they be in the family or on the soccer field or spiritually or otherwise," he said. "Everyday is a great opportunity."

When you set a goal, you must be the one who evaluates it. If you want to be able to juggle the ball 100 times without it touching the ground, you find it most difficult to accomplish that goal in one day. If you can juggle the ball once and strive to improve the number of juggles by one each day, in a little more than three months, you could juggle the ball 100 times.

He adheres to the old saying that "how you train is how you play in the game."

"You put the work in during the weeks, and the games will take care of themselves," Rote emphasized. "I think our guys believe that. You don't try to acquire new skills on game days, you just relax and use what talent you've been able to develop in previous games and practices."

Self-confidence is a most important factor in playing well. "To be able to hit a ball past a goalkeeper, you've got to believe you can do it. You've got to almost visually in your mind see yourself doing that," Rote said. "A lot of confident, competent players believe then can always score, they can always execute a pass properly or dribble past certain people. It does not mean their personal worth is any better, but they are certainly more confident athletes."

Daily practice can help increase your confidence. The more times you can shoot the ball into the back of the net during practice, make a perfect pass, or head a ball to a teammate's feet, the more confident you will be of repeating the same success in a game.

After you have practiced some skill or tactic during practice, then visualize yourself doing it perfectly in your mind. The more you concentrate on perfecting a skill or tactic in your mind, the better you will perform it in a game.

"Any time you can encompass your senses with your mind, you're better off," Rote said. "If you can see the crowd, feel the grass, the better you can put yourself into that scenario, the more realistic your image will be, and the more positive results you'll have in games."

One imaginary method some players have used can be played outdoors. Dribble across a field, park, or backyard. Imagine a tree is a defender and dribble around him. Imagine yourself making great moves during a game. The deeper your concentration, the better your playing in a game. There are unlimited little games you can make up and play.

Part of Rote's attitude toward soccer is that he wants his opponent to play well. "I guess from a spiritual perspective, it's important to me that every person, whether he's a soccer player or not, is able to operate in his life, lead a fulfilled life, enjoy himself, and learn to deal with himself," he explained. "So from really two standpoints, I'm concerned about my opponent. One is that if he plays well, he's going to force me to play better and that makes the game more competitive, and hopefully, give the fans a better game to enjoy. The second point is from a person to person basis. I enjoy seeing people succeed and do well and have a good self-image. That doesn't mean I say, 'here, take the ball'. When another player and I compete against each other and really play honest, fair, clean, and well, I'm very happy for him because it's an accomplishment that shows he's taken a lot of preparation and taken a lot of work. You have to have a level of respect for it."

Before a game he makes it a practice to shake the hand of the player who will be marking him during the game. If a player plays dirty against him, Rote will not seek revenge. "If I were to start yelling and lose my concentration, then I'm going to forget what I want to do offensively and defensively, and other things. It's up to the referee to sort out fouls and all those kinds of problems."

He always prays before each game. "In my prayer I want players to avoid injury, everyone to play well, and I want fans to have a good time," he said. "I want it (the game) to be an uplifting experience for everybody concerned, which doesn't mean that I don't want to win because I sure do."

Steve Wegerle
Tampa Bay Rowdies

Although many of today's athletes are trying to improve their games by changing the traditional method of playing their particular sport or position, Steve Wegerle of the Tampa Bay Rowdies has found that the old way of playing winger works best for him.

"If you have three strikers all together in the middle, everything is crowded. By having a winger who is playing wide, it opens up your forward line and their defense," he said. "They've got to push people out wide to mark the winger which creates a little bit more space in the middle."

Wegerle has played winger ever since he first started playing soccer when he was seven years old in Pretoria, South Africa where he was born on May 15, 1953. At age 10 he played on his first youth team, which was part of the Arcadia Shepherds professional soccer club's youth program. He also earned a starting position on his grammer school's top-ranked soccer team.

When he entered high school at age twelve, Wegerle found the school's athletic program included cricket and field hockey but no soccer so he continued his soccer with his Arcadia team. When he was fifteen, Wegerle's talent was recognized by Shepherd officials and he was promoted to the club's first team. Wegerle also captained the South African National Youth Team in 1969.

Wegerle credits his attitude for his early achievements. "I just really enjoy the sport. I probably took it more seriously than any of the other sports, like cricket or field hockey," he said. "I was probably more determined to do well in soccer. I used to work a lot harder at it than the other sports, too."

While he could have signed a professional contract and received all the economic benefits the other first team players did, his father wanted him to play on an amateur basis until he completed high school. He took his father's advice and played under an amateur contract until he finished high school at age eighteen. Since South Africa requires military service for all eighteen-year-old males, Wegerle spent the next year in the army.

When he left the army in 1972, Wegerle signed a professional contract and played with Arcadia until July, 1975, when he had an opportunity to play soccer in Holland. He convinced the Shepherds to loan him to the Dutch for a year and when the year was up, the Dutch wanted Wegerle to stay. But Arcadia still had his contract and demanded he return to Pretoria. Because of FIFA rules Wegerle had no choice but to return to the Shepherds and play for them.

About a year later, then-Tampa Bay coach, Eddie Firmani went to his native South Africa for a visit and saw Wegerle play. Searching for talent like Wegerle for the Rowdies, Firmani negotiated a contract release with Arcadia and brought Wegerle to Tampa Bay for the 1977 season.

An instant success in the team and with the fans, Wegerle has played the last three seasons with the Rowdies scoring three goals and twenty-one assists in 1979, and expects to remain in Tampa Bay for many more seasons. He still returns to his native Pretoria during the off-season to see his family and friends. Last winter, he and teammate Mike Connell organized the first South African youth soccer program and were overwhelmed with the program's acceptance and everyone's enthusiasm for developing youth soccer as it is in the United States.

In his youth clinics, Wegerle always advises players to learn as much as they can. "The more correct things you learn when you're young, the more they stick into your game, and the better they will serve you in the years to come."

To play wing, you must be able to dribble the ball well. "My favorite situation is to get one-on-one with a defender, take him on, hopefully beat him, and then create something for the forwards in the middle. That is really satisfying, especially if it leads to a goal being scored," Wegerle said.

A good winger will always evaluate his opponent early on in the first few minutes of a game. "I want to find out early which side he's weak on, the right or left, and how fast he is," Wegerle explained. "If a defender is slow, the easiest and the best way to beat him is to knock the ball by him and race for it. That's the easiest and least-complicated. That's the way I prefer to use, if it's possible. If he's fast, then you've got to work on faking him, getting him off balance by your body movements, and using your speed to get by him before he recovers."

If you are dribbling down the right wing and the fullback comes at you, drop your left shoulder, throw all your weight on the left hand side, and step over the ball with your left foot. If he watches your body and moves left in the direction your body is going, you knock the ball to the right with your right foot. Because your opponent is going to your left, he is too off-balance to recover and move in the opposite direction before you knock the ball past him and race onto it, according to Wegerle.

"It's all done in a split second," he noted. "But if the defender doesn't follow the way my body is going to the left, if he anticipates something and goes to my right, I'm still going left. I have time to change my move and just continue left, the way I was headed initially."

Another way to fake the defender is to feint a pass. When you get within four to five yards of the fullback, pull back your foot as though you are going to kick the ball in his direction. The natural thing for him to do is turn his back or protect his face with his arms. The moment he does that, you knock the ball past him and speed onto it before he has time to realize you were only faking him.

"Everything you do on the field happens in fractions of seconds," Wegerle said. "You've got to decide what you're going to do in a fraction of a second, and then do it."

Steve Wegerle (7)

If a fullback comes at you in stride, face-to-face, his legs may be open enough for you to knock the ball through between them for a nutmeg. Because he has to turn 180 degrees to chase you, you have time to run past him, control the ball, and continue dribbling down the field.

Another way to beat a fullback when you are running with the ball at him is to step over the ball with your left foot, keeping in stride, and then knock the ball ahead with your right foot.

"In other words, I step over the ball continuing in the same direction I am running, just over the ball with my left leg and bring my right leg behind my left leg, and knock the ball into the path that I am going with my right foot," Wegerle explained. "You will probably put the defender off stride, off balance, because he's not anticipating the ball to keep moving in the same direction. In the second he hesitates to see what you're going to do, you speed past him before he can react."

Another dribbling technique Wegerle uses is to dribble toward the fullback, slow down and then accelerate. When you slow down, the fullback may relax an instant, resting on his heels rather than being alert on his toes. If you catch him flat-footed, it takes him longer to recover than if he is positioned to move either way on his toes. The moment he relaxes, you sprint past him with the ball.

If a defender tries to slide tackle you, chip the ball 9 to 15 inches up so that his legs go underneath the ball. "I won't just knock it ahead on the ground because he's got a chance to get his foot in the way. Instead, I will just get my toe underneath it a little and chip it up over his leg, and then continue on."

Sometimes when you dribble down the touchline, you can fake by keeping the ball close to your foot. Although a good defender will mark you tight, he will not try to tackle the ball away when it is close to your foot because of the probability of missing the tackle when you have the ball under control. If you give him the impression that you have lost control of the ball, the defender might commit himself and dive for the ball. To induce him to commit, kick the ball a little ahead of you, just far enough ahead that it appears you have lost control for that second. If he tries to tackle, you have to sprint and get the ball before he does. If the defender makes a desperate dive for the ball, you have to sprint and regain control of the ball before he can tackle it away. If you are successful, your opponent will be too off-balance to recover for several seconds.

Wegerle explained you usually will have better success in running with the ball at a defender rather than slowing down. Speed dribbling gives you the advantage because the defender has no time to control you; he has to react to your attack. If you dribble slowly, the defender has time to decide whether he will commit himself, try to channel you to the left or right, or some other maneuver. Of course, if you slow down to get him to relax on his heels, then your technique is proper.

When Wegerle dribbles down the side of the field, he does not try to cross the ball from just anywhere along the way. "Once I beat my defender, I try most of all to go down as close to the goal line as possible and pull the ball back to a point about even with the penalty spot. Then I curl the ball back ten or twelve yards to my forwards. Curling the ball back makes it easier for them to head or kick the ball because they are running at the goal. The defenders are at a disadvantage because they have to head or kick the ball the other way," he explained. "I think this is the most dangerous play a winger can do."

During practice sessions, Wegerle frequently dribbles the ball down the wing with one forward running toward the near post and another forward going to the far post. This gives Wegerle a choice of either playing the ball over the top to the far post or short back to the near post. He has mastered such accuracy that he can cross the ball right to his teammate's forehead.

"When I get by the fullback and make the cross, I know somebody will be there," Wegerle said. "The better service from me, the easier it's going to be for the forward to score. So I always try and make it as easy as possible on my forwards."

In making the cross, he prefers a harder shot than a soft floater. "The harder shot is better because it doesn't give goalkeepers much time to get out, cut the ball out, and catch it," Wegerle said. "If a defender comes out and challenges me, gets right in front of me, I may have to curl it around him so that he does not obstruct it."

If his forwards and the opposing forwards are crowded together in front of the goal, making it difficult to pick out his teammates and accurately cross the ball to one of them, Wegerle will probably drive the ball hard and low into the goalmouth, hoping a teammate will kick it or a defender will deflect it into the goal.

When you dribble down the wing, always be aware of everything going on around you. "Because your concentration is centered on beating your fullback and getting the ball past him and getting a good cross in, a lot of the time your head is down watching the ball and watching your opponent," Wegerle observed. "The more you can be aware of what is going on around you, who's free, and where the different players are, the better you'll be able to hit good balls in less time."

If he dribbles down the wing and sees one of his forwards free or in position to take a shot on goal, Wegerle will immediately cross the ball to him. If nobody in the middle is free or in shooting position, Wegerle will continue dribbling down the touchline to give them more time to get free. As soon as one of them breaks loose, he crosses the ball to him.

He rarely tries to shoot on goal from the wing. "It's very difficult because most of the time you are at an acute angle. The chances of you beating the goalkeeper from twenty-five to thirty yards out at that angle are slim," Wegerle noted. "Usually, a half-decent goalkeeper won't let any in. If I do happen to come inside across the box, then I most certainly will take a shot."

An example of when he would come inside occurs when he is one-on-one with the defender at the edge of the eighteen-yard box. If he beats him on the inside and has a chance to score, then he will shoot. If there is a crowd of players in front of the goal blocking his shot, he will pass back or to a teammate in the vicinity of the far post.

During the entire game, Wegerle concentrates on beating the opponent marking him and creating chances for his forwards. "I get a lot of satisfaction creating goals, as much as I do by scoring them," he said.

Players must communicate with each other throughout

the entire game. "If I make a run inside, I'm talking to my fullbacks or the midfielder on my side of the field to go up wide on my side where I have just run from," he explained. "I'm talking to my players all the time. If I see something nobody else does, I'll tell them about it right away."

Off-the-ball movement is important for a winger just as it is for a forward playing inside. If his fullback dribbles the ball up the line behind him, Wegerle will make a run into the middle of the field, hoping that the opponent marking him will follow and leave an open space for the fullback with the ball to run into.

Square passes, passing in a straight line perpendicular to the touchline, should be avoided in your team's half of the field. "If the ball gets cut out by one of the opposing team, then you're really in big trouble," Wegerle explained. "I think you'd only really use the square pass around the opposing team's goal, where you're cutting the ball into the middle."

He prefers to pass the ball on the ground rather than in the air because it is easier for his teammate to control it. If he has to trap the ball with his head, chest, or thigh, he has less time to play the ball before an opponent tries to tackle it away.

Wingers usually do not have very many chances to pass the ball back to midfielders behind them. One instance you might pass back would occur if you had your back to the goal line and a defender marked you tight from behind. Another opportunity would arise if he dribbled to the midfield line and a midfielder was in position behind you to take a shot on goal.

Crossing the ball from one side of the field to the other can be a most effective play. "If the ball is being played on your right hand side of the field, the chances are that seventy to eighty percent of the players are drawn slightly over to right where the ball is," Wegerle said. "Obviously, there is going to be a lot of space over on the left side. If one of your players makes a run on the far side, you can cross the ball to him. 'Switch play' we call it. It causes a lot of problems to the opposing team because they've got to move from the right side over to the man who has the ball now on the far side."

Use switch-passes only in the opposing team's half of the field. Avoid switch passes in your team's half of the field because if you make a bad cross or an opponent cuts the ball out, then your team is in trouble.

If you make a long pass or cross, avoid kicking it too high. "The harder and lower you hit it, the quicker it will get there and the less time the other team has to react to it," Wegerle advised. "It should just be high enough to get over their heads."

Corner kicks should also be hit hard and just high enough to pass over the defenders' heads. "By giving it a good crisp shot, it makes it harder for opposing defenders and goalkeepers to handle the ball," he said. "If you're just going to kick a high ball into the middle, it gives them time to position themselves and it's easier for the goalkeeper to handle."

Before your team takes a corner kick, one of your taller and stronger players should be at the far post and another striker at the near post. If you kick the ball right to the player at the near post, he has two options. He can try to head it into the goal or flick it across the goalmouth to the far post for the other striker to head into the goal. If the ball is hit to the player at the far post, he also has two options. He can head it into the goal or flick it off to a teammate who might be in a better shooting position.

"We know exactly what we're going to do because we work on it (corner kicks) everyday in training," Wegerle said.

Whether you hit the ball to the striker at the far or near post depends on your players' strengths. "If you don't have any tall, strong strikers, then you will have to find another way. Work on a corner kick that fits your players," he said.

Before you take the corner kick, look around so you have a mental picture of where everyone is. If you want to hit it to the striker at the near post, strike the ball with the inside of the foot so that it will go toward the penalty spot and then curl in a C-shape to the near post.

If you hit it to the striker positioned at the far post, then you kick it straight over everybody in the penalty area to your teammate, rather than curling it.

"It's got to be right over to the far post, out of the goal-keeper's reach," Wegerle said. "It's really useless dropping it in right in the middle of the penalty area because there are so many people there that the chances of somebody doing something with it are slim. Knock it all the way over everybody in the middle for one of your big chaps at the far post. As the ball goes over, everybody in the box turns around and follows it. The big chap can knock it straight back into the middle. By doing that, everybody is a little confused, not as ready for the ball as they were before I took the corner kick. When the big chap flicks it into the middle, one of your players who knows what is happening can try to head it in."

You can use a short-corner kick, if everyone is tightly marked in the middle in front of the goalmouth. By playing it short to a midfielder, you draw some of the opposing defenders out toward you which opens up the defense. The midfielder can hit it the first time into the middle to your strikers, take a shot himself if he has a scoring opportunity, or pass it back to you for a cross.

"Try to get the ball in there as soon as you can," Wegerle said. "Use the space creatively."

Corner kicks do not require brute power. "If you strike it with correct timing, it'll go as far and as straight as you want it to," he emphasized. "Some people think if a player has really big legs and he is very strong and muscular, he should really be able to kick a ball far. It doesn't work like that. It depends entirely on his timing. Of course, a really big, strong person who has good timing is going to kick it farther and harder than a skinny chap with good timing."

"You should work a lot on crosses," Wegerle advised. "If you have done a lot of hard work in getting past your defender and then you happen to cross the ball behind the goal, all your good work you put in to get past the defender is wasted. Work on your crosses until you are able to cross the ball well."

One error wingers sometimes make is coming into the middle of the field when they are not in the opposing team's goal area. You should play wide to help keep the players in the middle spread out. You will also be more open to receive passes and create scoring opportunities. When you are in the opposing team's end of the field, you definitely want to come inside when you have the opportunity to assist or make a goal.

One drill Wegerle recommends for wingers to use for improving ball control involves placing several cones or markers in a straight line about twenty yards apart. Dribble as fast as you can through the cones and then pass the ball to a teammate who is moving around so you do not always know where he is. This forces you to keep your head up and look around while dribbling. Time yourself to see how long it takes you to dribble in and out of the cones and then work on reducing that time. The better your ball control and the faster your speed, the better winger you will be.

To become the best player you can, you must be dedicated. "If you want to be good and reach the top, you've got to dedicate yourself to that sport, and work at it all the time. If you don't have dedication, you may as well forget about it. You might get halfway there on natural ability, but you won't get any farther. You've really got to have dedication," Wegerle advised.

"Play to win all the time. Never give up, even when you're behind in a game. You've got to battle to get where you want to go."

Alan Willey
Minnesota Kicks

Nicknamed the "Artful Dodger" by his teammates, center forward Alan Willey can dribble past a host of defenders to pass to a teammate or shoot with amazing accuracy. He also is known for being able to turn and shoot in one swift motion, capitalizing on seemingly impossible opportunities.

In 1979, he was ranked eighth among the top NASL scorers and holds the Minnesota Kicks club record for the number of hat tricks, two-goal games, points and shots. While he is known as a top forward in the game, Willey has not always played on the front line.

Born in Houghton LeSpring, England on October 18, 1956, Willey played for his first school team at age six and was made the team's goalkeeper. He minded the nets for two years until he was stricken with meningitis and spent three months in the hospital.

When he recuperated, Willey and his family moved to a new neighborhood where he found the school team already had a goalkeeper. "I tried playing forward because I just wanted to play soccer. That's all I ever wanted to do."

His physical education teacher helped Willey to refine his skills and counseled him about his future in soccer. "He always took me aside and gave me a few tips. I took his advice and that's where I am today."

By the time he reached fifteen, Willey played for his school and the local YMCA, which meant every Saturday, he played two games. When he was sixteen, a scout for Middlesbrough saw him score two goals in a YMCA game and two weeks later Willey received a letter inviting him to try out for the first-division professional soccer club.

The first tryout was held on a Sunday afternoon. In a game of three twenty-minute periods, he scored a hat trick (three goals) in the first period. Asked to return to the second tryout game, he scored another hat trick. Willey then accepted a Middlesbrough apprenticeship.

He found the life of an apprentice held little of the glory of a professional soccer player. "You don't play much soccer," Willey said. "You sort of work around the grounds, train all morning, sweep up after the games on Saturday, clean boots and the locker rooms, and get the stands ready for the next game."

After nine months, he was promoted to the reserve team and signed a professional contract. In 1975 after playing a couple of games for the reserve team, Willey advanced to the first team.

At the end of the British soccer season in the spring of 1976, Willey was loaned to the Minnesota Kicks of the NASL where he scored sixteen goals and became the team's leading scorer. He returned to Middlesbrough that fall, played the British soccer season, and came back to the Kicks on loan for the 1977 NASL season. That year he led the Kicks with fourteen goals. Willey proved himself such an asset for Minnesota that the club purchased his contract from Middlesbrough. He scored twenty-one goals and had three assists in 1978, ranking him sixth among the leading scorers for that season.

Willey plays most of the game in the opposing team's eighteen-yard box, scoring most of his goals from the six-yard box area. He usually has his back to the opponents' goal so he can receive passes from his midfielders. When a midfielder plays a ball to his feet, Willey may fake to the left to get the defender behind him off-balance, then push the ball to his right, turn quickly, and shoot.

"The way you turn depends on which side the ball comes to you. If it's too far left, you won't try to turn to the right side because it would be difficult," he said. "If the ball comes more to the right, I fake to the left, and then turn to the right. If the defender has taken your fake and moved to your left, the space on the right is already open when you run and shoot."

Know where the defender is behind you. If he is standing to your left behind you, turn with the ball to your right, unless your fake caused him to move to your right. If he is behind you to your right, turn left.

"Keep your arms not outstretched, but bent at the elbows so you can feel the defender. If he marks you tight, he will bump against your hand or arm," Willey said. "After you've got enough playing experience, you'll be able to know when a defender is coming in, how he's coming in. You just sort of sense where he is."

If you keep your arms out from your body, the defender will find it difficult to get around you when the midfielder passes you the ball.

When the ball is passed to you, you must be able to turn it either with the inside or outside of your foot. You also should be able to turn the ball with either your right or left foot. If a defender knows you can only turn the ball with your right foot, he will make your turning more difficult, according to Willey.

"When the ball comes to you, the closer you can stop the ball and the closer you can keep it near you, the less chance the defender has of pinching it off you," he said. "You've got to cushion it."

If the ball is passed to you on your right, lean to the left trying to fake the defender into moving in that direction. Control the ball with the inside of your right foot, put the sole of your foot on the ball, roll it backward away from the defender. He will rush through and miss the ball, giving you an opportunity to shoot or pass it off to someone.

"If you've got good control, a defender is going to struggle trying to get the ball away from you. The better your control, the more time you're going to have," Willey explained. "If you haven't got good control, you're going to find people coming in, sticking their feet in trying to get the ball away from you. The better your control, the better the player you're going to be.

"When you turn with the ball, try to turn as quick as possible, but not so quick that you get the ball stuck beneath your feet. If that happens and you panic, you'll lose the ball. Just keep your eye on the ball and try to do it as easy and fast as you can," Willey said.

The best way to learn how to turn is to practice by yourself. Practice controlling the ball with the inside and outside of both feet. Start out easy and then increase your pace until you can turn the ball quickly. When you feel confident enough, have a defender mark you from behind and try to steal the ball away. You both will benefit from this practice.

If you turn quickly and find a defender facing you, fake him by moving your foot like you are going to kick the ball out wide. When he sticks his leg out to block the pass, push the ball through his legs (nutmeg), run around him and regain control of the ball. Because the defender is off-balance with his leg stretched out, it will be difficult for him to recover for a second or two.

If the defender is marking you very tight when you receive the ball from the midfielder, you may want to dribble forward a yard and then turn to take him on one-on-one.

Another fake is make the defender think you plan to pass the ball back to the midfielder. "If the ball is coming at a nice pace, let it pass through you," Willey said. "The defender thinks you're going to stop it and he's not ready for the ball when it goes past him. Then you turn around and shoot. That's been successful for me."

If a teammate plays the ball in about knee high, you can catch it on the volley, flick it over your head and the defender, turn quickly and take a shot. Flick the ball up just high enough to clear the defender's head and land behind him. If you flick the ball up too high, the defender has enough time to turn around and compete for the ball.

When a ball is passed to him in the air, Willey prefers to shoot on the volley before the ball hits the ground rather than on a half volley after the ball has hit the ground.

"You're going to have more chance to score a goal with

Alan Willey (9)

a volley because when you volley the ball, it can dip or curl in the goal. If you hit the ball on a half-volley, you hit the ball farther, but the line of the ball is going to be true, in a straight line. It's not going to dip or rise like a volley," Willey explained. "The goalkeeper or defender who is on the goal line just has to get himself in for the shot coming on the half-volley. It's easier for him to see than when a volleyed ball is moving in the air."

Willey uses his instep to hit the volley. "With the instep, you really get a good whack at it. The ball is really going to move about," he said. "If you hit with the side of your foot, you can't get any power behind it."

The amount of power you want in your kick depends on how far away from the goal you are. If you are on the eighteen-yard line, you want to use power to beat the goal-keeper. If you are about twelve yards out or less, use the inside of your foot for accuracy. If the goalkeeper is too far out in front of the goal, try and chip the ball over him.

One common error young forwards make is trying to hit the ball too hard. "You just strike the ball nicely and try to place it," Willey said. "If you try to bust the leather, the ball is going to go over the bar or bobble and the goalkeeper is just going to pick it up. Don't waste the shot by trying to kick it too hard."

One way to beat the goalkeeper in a one-on-one situation is the "dummy." Fake like you are going to shoot into the left side of the goal. At the same time the goalkeeper moves left to block your shot, you push the ball to the right hand side of the goal. If the goalkeeper is moving left, he may be too far off-balance to recover and save your shot.

Whenever a goalkeeper runs toward you, take your shot before he can stop or slow down. Keep your shot low because he is usually too off-balance to make a good dive, Willey said.

When Willey is in a crowd of players in front of the goal and the ball is crossed from the wing, he times his run to the goalmouth so he is in front of the defender marking him when the ball comes into the penalty area.

"I stand about a yard behind the player who is marking me so he can't see me when the winger is ready to cross the ball," he said. "I start my run behind him so he can't see me coming, and if he can't see me coming, I'm going to get a yard start on him. I just run past him. Since he's coming from a standing position, it's hard to catch me," Willey said.

When you make your run, be sure you stay onsides. Some

defenders will not follow you into the six-yard box because they expect the goalkeeper to cover that area. If you are caught with only the goalkeeper between you and the goal, you will be called offsides.

If you are marked tightly by a defender who stymies every scoring opportunity for you, drop back deep into the mid-field area. Because some defenders prefer to stay in their own position area, they will not follow you out beyond their 35-yard line. Another way is to beat them almost every time when you get the ball. This will discourage them, and perhaps decrease their effectiveness.

If you find your game is off, the defender successfully tackles you every time you get the ball, and a wave of depression hits you, then go back to basics.

"You might be trying some hard things which are not coming off. So go back to the easiest way to control the ball. Play everything as easy as you can until you regain your confidence," Willey advised. "If you've lost the ball two or three times when you've tried to turn with it, lay it back to the midfielder when he knocks it to you. When your confidence is back up, try to turn again and beat the defender."

On corner kicks, Willey usually runs to the near post. If the ball comes into his area, he will head the ball to the far post. "Try and flick the ball on to the far post for your teammate to head in. You don't want to get too much contact on the ball or it will just go straight up in the air or back to the fellow who took the corner kick," he explained. "Just let it glance off the top of your head, right above the forehead."

You should try to head the ball into the net from the near post only when the goalkeeper is out of position. Because the goalkeeper is usually ready to block any head shot from the near post, it is better to pass it to a teammate at the far post. Then rush into the middle in case the ball gets knocked down or the goalkeeper drops it.

If you see the corner kick is a long pass to the far post, try to lure defenders to the near post and away from your teammate at the far post. When the ball comes overhead, turn around, and race into the center for any scoring opportunity that comes your way.

If you are running with the ball from twenty yards out, keep your eye on the ball. "If you're running and you take your eye off the ball, it could bobble away from you or run too far ahead of you. You might look at the goal and miskick it all together. So you've got to keep your eye on the ball," Willey said. "If you've been playing for a while, you know where the goal is so you don't have to look at it. You try and get your shot off as quickly as possible, without trying to rush your shot. If you're going to snatch at the ball, then you're going to miskick it.

Every player should work on his ball control. "There is always room for improvement," Willey said. "Juggle the ball, see how many times you can keep it up. That's good ball control training. Then get a friend to knock a few balls at you at various heights and try to control them."

Shooting drills are also important. Willey practices shooting for fifteen to twenty minutes every day. One drill he likes calls for the forward with the ball to start at the thirty-five-yard line. You pass the ball to the player standing in front of you about twenty yards out from the goal. When you run toward the goal, he lays the ball off to your right or left for you to shoot into the goal. Start off with a goalkeeper in goal but no defender. Add a defender later when you are warmed up.

"If the defender is a long way from you when you reach the ball, you can take time to control it before you shoot," Willey said. "Don't try to dribble or control it, if the defender is close by. You've got to hit it first time or you may lose the scoring opportunity."

To improve your dribbling, he recommends a drill where you have three or four rows of cones. Each row consists of four or more cones about five feet apart. Assign three or four players to each row. Then have each team dribble one at a time through the cones as fast as they can to see which team wins.

"I think that helps you, especially when you play up front," Willey said. "After a breakaway, you sometimes have to beat two or three defenders before you can shoot, so you have to be able to dribble through them."

Willey attributes his success to being in the right place at the right time. "I work hard at training. I work on things I'm not very good at. When I first started I wasn't too good at turning but I practiced until now I'm pretty good at it. Always try to improve the things you're good at and turn your weaknesses into strengths," Willey advised.

Part Two

The Midfielders

Rick Davis
New York Cosmos

Rick Davis is believed by many to be the first American-born soccer superstar. After only two years of college soccer at Santa Clara University, Davis was signed by the NASL Champion New York Cosmos, where he earned a starting position as a midfielder and sometimes forward in 1979.

Born on November 24, 1958, Davis started playing soccer at age six in Claremont, California about the time the American Youth Soccer Organization (AYSO) was being developed. He also played baseball, football, and tennis.

"In looking at all the other sports, there were too many constant breaks in the action," Davis said. "I really enjoyed continually running around and being part of the game, even though I did not always have the ball. I also enjoyed the challenge of using my feet whereas in other sports you use your hands. Since it's easier to use your hands than it is to use your feet, I guess I just enjoyed the challenge of playing soccer."

He dreamed about becoming a professional athlete almost from the time he entered grammar school. "At the time soccer wasn't really big enough that I really set soccer in my mind as being the sport I wanted to play. I was also indecisive about the other sports," Davis said. "But when I got to be about nine or ten and saw the development and growth of soccer over just those three years, I anticipated that someday it would be big and that I could, if I were good enough, play soccer professionally. Although, I didn't ever think that I was going to be good enough. I just hoped that someday something magical would happen and I would be good enough."

After he had made his decision to become a professional soccer player, he played and practiced an average of six hours a day, from the time he was about nine until he signed with the Cosmos.

"Even in high school when I was playing other sports, after we finished practice there, a lot of us would shower, get dressed and put on our soccer shoes, and then go to the park near my home and play a couple of games with a soccer ball."

Davis played four years of varsity soccer at Damien High School. He credits Al Mistri, his soccer coach at Damien, for developing him as a player and a person. "He instilled in me a competitiveness, a proper attitude about the game, and then gave me a basic overview of what I needed to do to learn to play the game." He and Coach Mistri often stayed after practice and worked on Davis' shooting and other techniques long after everyone else had gone home.

After graduating from high school, he entered his freshman year at Santa Clara University where he played varsity soccer. "Coach Dave Chaplik showed me a different aspect of the game," Davis said. "He helped me gain the proper attitude for playing college soccer, and I owe quite a bit to Dave for that."

When the Cosmos offered Davis a contract to sign with the club after his sophomore year at Santa Clara, Davis decided to leave college and joined the Cosmos on an amateur basis. Under NASL rules and regulations, he also has a fully paid scholarship for when he returns to college.

In high school he was named All-America in 1975 and again in 1976. He was selected for the United States National Youth Team in 1976 and played in the CONCACAF Games. Davis was one of two Americans named to the CONCACAF All-Star Team.

In 1977 Coach Walt Chyzowych selected him for the United States National Team and United States Olympic Team. In March, 1978 he captained the United States Olympic "B" Team which won the Bellinzona Easter Tournament

Rick Davis (17)

in Switzerland. After he signed with the Cosmos, he trained during the 1977-78 off-season with A.C. Milan, a top team in the Italian first division. After the 1979 season, Davis turned professional and signed a two-year contract with the New York club.

While he now plays attacking midfielder for the Cosmos, he played center forward from the time he joined his first AYSO team. He has played center forward and midfielder for the United States National Team.

Davis thinks that every soccer player should play every position on the field for a better understanding of the game. Not only will you gain the experience of how a forward, midfielder, or defender plays his game, but you will also learn how a player thinks in playing each position. This knowledge will better enable you to play against a forward or defender or midfielder when you return to your regular position. You may even find out that you play another position better than the one you play now.

"The only person who should specialize might be the goalkeeper, but even he should know the field players positions," Davis said. "It's great for forwards to gain experience playing fullback because you learn what you as a defender like or don't like for a forward to do during the game. If you're a defender and you play forward, you get to know what a defender does that might bother a forward."

The midfielder must know how to both attack and defend. When the opposing team gets the ball down into your back third of the field and their forwards outnumber your defenders, the midfielders should race back and become fullbacks until your team gets the ball forward. When your team is on the attack, you support the offensive players. If there are three forwards against four defenders, you become the fourth attacker. If a fellow midfielder joins the attack, your offense now has the advantage of five on four.

"They're (midfielders) there to try and draw some cohesiveness between fullbacks and forwards, a link between the two. The attacking midfielder is one of the best weapons a team can have."

Many teams assign their defenders to mark a specific forward. Since a midfielder usually will not mark his opposing midfielder as tight as a right fullback will mark a left winger, the attack midfielder can be very dangerous in the opponents' end of the field.

"A lot of times, the midfielder coming through or making a run up the field can find himself open for a pass or cross," Davis explained. "That's why he is often the one who does the scoring for the team."

While a fullback has to watch what is happening in front of

him and a forward has to be alert of everything going on behind him, the midfielder must be aware of what is happening both in front and in back of him.

"The midfielder has to comprehend what's going on at all times. He must have very good vision, in other words, he has to know where all the players are and read the game so he can anticipate what will happen next."

During the first fifteen minutes of the game, the midfielder must evaluate both teams' strengths and weaknesses as well as the midfielder he is playing against. "I'm looking to see which one of their fullbacks is the weakest and which of our attackers seems to be doing the best against the other team," Davis said.

Watch to see if your right winger is able to consistently beat the left fullback marking him and cross the ball or bring it inside. Or is the fullback capable of preventing the winger from bringing the ball down the side, either by forcing him to pass the ball or tackling it away from him? Is your center forward marked so tight by the center back and sweeper that he has no opportunity to get the ball or can he maneuver around his opponents into open space for a pass or cross? Do your midfielders dominate the middle of the field or do theirs? Is your right fullback breaking up the left winger's attack every time he tries to dribble the ball down to cross it or is the winger beating him three out of five times? Does your center back dominate the opposing forward in the air? You must assess the answers to these questions and others right away.

"You want to know exactly what match-ups are in your favor, forward versus defender, and what match-ups are in the other team's favor, especially if you're the playmaker," Davis said. "Play the ball to your strengths or the ones that are in your favor, and away from the other team's strengths."

If your right winger consistently beats his fullback, feed the ball to him. If their right fullback dominates your left winger, do not play the ball to him. If your right fullback is having problems with their left winger, then you may have to help him out sometimes.

"If you're the playmaker and you notice that the other

team tends to leave their right side exposed, and the ball is not really near that area, what I like to do is kind of play the ball away from that area until all of a sudden you get someone to run into that open space. Then change the ball to him right away; therefore, giving us the advantage," Davis explained. "That's what the game is all about, gaining advantage one way or the other, and then ultimately capitalizing on either the other team's mistakes or your good plays, your intelligent playing."

One play a team can work on is to have the wingers move inside toward the edge of the penalty area, drawing their fullbacks with them. Then your right and left midfielders or fullbacks move up into the open spaces on the wings. Then play the ball to the open teammate on either wing for him to cross or bring it inside.

"The communication comes in your understanding of the game," Davis said. "You and your teammates all have to see the same weaknesses and the same openings as a team, and then all of you make the same adjustments. You develop this kind of teamwork and communication through practicing, playing, and working together as a cohesive team."

When you evaluate the other team's style of play during the first fifteen minutes of the game, see whether they like to dribble a lot or pass after one or two touches on the ball, make short or long passes, play everything slow and easy or at a really fast-paced running game.

"As a playmaker you want to control the game. You want to control the tempo, the speed of the game. If the other team is playing faster than you are used to normally playing, then you try and slow the game down. Play the ball around in the midfield, but not really going anywhere. Pass the ball back, up and then back, so you're keeping the pace very slow," Davis said.

If you are playing against a team that likes to play the ball slowly in a deliberate style of play, then speed the game up. Play all your balls quickly and forward. Force them to speed up their game.

You can gain the element of surprise by changing the tempo of the game. If the other team has been playing a slow, deliberate game, you can throw them off by speeding the game up. In the few seconds they take to recover and adjust to the fast tempo, your team can take advantage of the situation and possibly score a goal. If your team has been working hard and your teammates have been making a lot of runs up and down field, slow the game down for a time to give them a rest.

"The playmaker controls the style of the game as well as the tempo," he said. "You dictate to your team how we want the game played. Always play to your team's strengths by reading how the other team is playing and their weaknesses. Some playmakers' styles are so unpredictable that they often keep the other team off-balance because they never know what to expect."

Always be alert to turn the other team's attack into a counterattack. If the opposing forwards and midfielders attack your goal and you win the ball away from them, look immediately for a teammate who is open in the opponents' half of the field. Without hesitation, pass the ball to him before the other team can recover and set up a defense. "You're speeding up the tempo of the game," Davis said. "As soon as you win it, your team should attack their goal."

Creativity is essential for every playmaker, according to Davis. One way to create a goal-scoring opportunity is to take advantage of the other team's mistakes. Another way is to do the unexpected. The element of surprise may give your team the few seconds it needs to put your opponents off-balance and get the ball into the back of their net.

Every soccer player should enjoy running, especially midfielders who run from one goal line to the other and back. In his youth soccer days, Davis enjoyed running so much that he could never get enough of it. "I was always running," he recalled. "When the soccer game was over, I would play tennis, and that evening I would go jogging with my father. I never had to learn how to enjoy running."

Aside from practicing ball skills, Davis realizes that mental preparation is important to his game performance and spends about fifteen minutes each night readying himself mentally for the next day's match.

"It (mental preparation) is an individual thing," he said. "For example, if I'm thinking of my strengths, like shooting, I usually visualize in my mind a ball rolling toward me. I look at my foot, plant it next to the ball, lock my ankle, and strike the ball directly in the middle with my shoelaces, making sure my knee is over it, and everything is right. I focus in on the point of impact and see the ball go in the back of the net.

"I think what happens in a game situation when the ball might be rolling toward me, or I might be taking a shot, my subconscious takes over and says, 'Hey, we've done this before, there you go,' and I hit the ball into the back of the net. In other words, envisioning myself kicking the ball the proper way, doing the proper technique, helps me score goals."

When he plays center forward for the United States National Team, Davis usually finds himself marked by a center back when the game starts. "Try a few things, like cutting to his left, then you see how he plays you," Davis said. "If he turns better to one side than the other, you try and go to his weak side. If you try a certain fake and it works out really well, you try a few more fakes, different moves. Sure, you're going to lose the ball early in the game, but it's more important early in the game to figure out what the guy's weaknesses are. Once you know how he reacts to different things and his weaknesses, you know how to play your strengths and the things he does the weakest."

In a one-on-one situation with a goalkeeper, watch him to see how he approaches you. If he misplays his angle some way where he leaves a larger part of the goal open on one side, try to slide the ball past him before he realizes his mistake. Avoid any hesitation when the goalkeeper comes off his line and approaches you. "The idea is to prepare yourself quickly once you have the ball," Davis advised. "Start looking for it, see what's actually going to happen when you have that encounter."

One way to fool a goalkeeper is to hit the ball with the toe of your shoe. When you are running with the ball at the goal, do not stop or wind up, just strike the ball with the toe of your shoe. If the goalkeeper is unprepared, you have a chance of scoring.

Another technique to beat the goalkeeper is to fake a shot. When you stride with the ball toward the goal, bring back one foot like you are winding up to take a shot, then suddenly stop or dig your cleats into the turf without hitting the ball. If the goalkeeper moves out of position, stops and hesitates, or dives down at the ball, you have a better opportunity to score.

Regardless of what position you play, always maintain a positive attitude toward your fellow teammates. "Let's say I make a bad pass and it goes out of bounds. Instead of a teammate saying, 'You idiot! What are you trying to do, you're no good, why didn't you give me the ball,' it would be much better for a teammate to say something positive and constructive, like 'better luck next time' or 'not quite so much power next time.' By saying something constructive, he's in essence explaining to me that he understands my mistake, but he's not putting me down in front of my teammates or the fans."

If you yell and criticize a player, he will probably yell and criticize you when you make a mistake. The emotional outbursts not only hamper teamwork, but can also strain your game concentration.

The same principle applies to coaches. While they have to tell players what they do wrong, they can criticize players in a constructive way with the result the players feel good about themselves and the coach.

"Do it the wrong way and you can have a terrible team. Be positive and constructive, and you can have a great team," Davis emphasized. "That goes for everyone."

Rodney Marsh
Tampa Bay Rowdies

Because Rodney Marsh has the talent and unique ability to flow with the pulse of the game rather than play a rigid position, his style of play is best described as spontaneous.

"I play a deep forward right behind the front striker, much like an inside right under the old system. I'm a ball holder, really like a quarterback," he explained. "My job is to pick up the ball from deep and spray passes around the field. There is no typical situation to describe the way I play because I'm a very spontaneous player."

Marsh has been a creative player ever since he first started playing soccer at about age four. Born in 1944 and raised in a tough neighborhood in London, England, Marsh played a lot of five-aside soccer with his friends in the streets and parks.

His father was probably the single most important influence on his career. "He was always very positive. He never doubted that I would be a professional. I think he molded me to become a soccer player," Marsh recalled. "I think he saw in me what he would have liked to have been himself."

Marsh's father was a talented amateur soccer player. He often watched his father play and emulated him when playing with his friends. He and dad also spent a lot of time together kicking the ball around and developing skills.

"My whole life was geared and pointed toward soccer," he said. "I had a pair of soccer boots from the time I could remember. I always had a soccer ball."

Marsh played on his first youth team at age ten, but he never received any real coaching until he became an apprentice professional. Everything he learned, he taught himself by watching others like his father and professionals playing in London.

He was always a goal-scorer. His most memorable youth soccer experience happened during a school game when he scored thirteen goals.

Marsh became an apprentice professional at age seventeen when he joined Fulham. He signed a professional contract upon becoming eighteen and went on to play for the Queens Park Rangers and Manchester United before returning to Fulham. He also played for the English National Team.

Because the style of play in those years was very rigid compared to the changing style of today, only one of his British professional coaches allowed Marsh to capitalize on his spontaneous style for scoring goals and creating goal scoring opportunities for teammates.

"Malcom Allison of Manchester United was the only coach who gave me license to do what I felt was right," Marsh recalled. "With all the other coaches I played under, there was always a kind of underlying coat of rigid regimentation to a certain degree, even though they were wrong."

Marsh came to Tampa Bay in 1976 and played with the Rowdies until the end of the 1979 season when he retired at the peak of his career. Playing under coach Gordon Jago, Marsh used his imagination and creativity to lead the team to two conference championships.

His positive attitude has been a key to his success and an inspiration to others. "I have very positive thoughts always. I try to gear my mind for winning at all times," Marsh said. "I am not a negative person. I tend to positiveness. I think about scoring goals and creating goals for other players all the time."

During a game, he runs a play through his mind before it happens. "I have a mental image of the play as it develops," Marsh explained. "I also have a mental image of what the outcome will be. For instance, the ball is on the right and I'm coming through the center. I try to make a mental image of the ball coming across into the penalty area and what I'm going to do when it gets there.

"This is something I trained myself to do. I find it's very important because if you have made an outlook on what is going to happen just before the incident is about to happen, then you're much better prepared to take advantage of the situation than the guy who is going to try and stop you. When the action actually happens, it's spontaneous. That's the reason why it is so successful and why it can help you a lot," Marsh said.

Because Marsh relies on his perceptions of the game more than on speed, he will often drift rather than race into open spaces where he knows he can receive a pass and play the ball. He also prefers to move around the field, from his own thirty-five-yard line to his opponents' goal, rather than remain stationary in one area.

Peripheral vision is also an important part of his game. Marsh keeps his head up, always looking around, alert to where everyone is and what they are doing. He is also one of the most skillful players in the League, especially in distributing and accurately passing the ball.

"Concentrate on keeping your eye on the ball. Make sure of the correct weight of the pass, don't overweight the pass too far, and underweight the pass," Marsh said.

He believes one of the best ways to develop passing accuracy is to kick a ball against a garage door. "Keep passing at the door until you become very accurate. Then take the ball further back, and instead of passing from twenty feet, pass it from thirty feet," he suggested. "When you become accurate at that distance, try to pass from forty feet. That's a very good way of going about it."

Pass the ball with the inside of the foot for the most accuracy. If you want power, use the instep kick. Anytime you have to pass the ball thirty yards or more, drive it with the instep. If you only need to pass the ball ten yards, use the inside of your foot.

"Point your foot in the direction you want the ball to go," Marsh said. "Keep your eye on the ball at all times and your body over the ball. That's very important."

Rodney Marsh (10)

When you want to pass the ball into open space in front of a teammate, you must be aware of his position and speed. If he is running fast, you obviously have to play it farther in front of him than if your teammate is standing still. Never pass the ball behind him. Always play the ball so he runs onto it without having to change speed or direction.

Marsh often disguised the direction of his passes by looking in the opposite direction of where he wanted to pass the ball. This technique may lessen the pressure on the intended receiver because the opponents focus their attention on the area where Marsh is looking. Then he passes the ball where he wants to.

Unless there is a lot of traffic, players standing between you and the teammate you want to pass to, Marsh recommends that you pass the ball on the ground rather than in the air, even if the distance is thirty yards or more.

"The ball takes a shorter time to get there on the ground than in the air. It's my technique," he said. "You have to be very accurate to pass on the ground. If you make a mistake, somebody will cut out the pass and mount a counterattack. So you have to be very accurate."

Marsh is known for his continuous talking during a game. "It's essential because you have to lead by example," he said, referring to being team captain. "I like to have everybody on the same wavelength as I am. If you're communicating all the time, they're always up and their minds don't wander."

Communicating a continuous flow of ideas during a game and giving encouragement to the players is an important part of the captain's job.

"Communication is essential during a game," Marsh explained. "The players know exactly where their teammates are. They know they're healthy, they're prepared to handle situations. If a team is quiet, the ball might go through it, somebody might leave it, somebody might get cut out, the ball might go to the other team."

Although opponents can hear instructions given back and forth among the Rowdies, they often do not comprehend their meaning because Tampa Bay uses a lot of rehearsed set plays.

"A typical set play would be when the ball is knocked to one of our forwards. He takes it and runs purposefully to me. Then he spins off, and runs behind me into the gap. I play the ball first time, like a decoy play, and I'll shout to him 'over,' meaning just leave it. He knows I am right behind him and so he leaves the ball for me to run onto," Marsh explained.

Besides being the team's morale booster during the game, the captain has to make the right decisions on and off the field. "I try to always keep our players under control, telling them not to lose their heads and get yellow or red cards." To achieve that, he sometimes finds it necessary to calm a player down and keep him separated from the referee or an opponent.

Socializing off the field, especially after games, helps keep up team morale. "We're always laughing and joking," he said. "If the spirit is good, then the team is good."

If a conflict arises between two players, it is best to work it out right away before their problem affects the team. As captain Marsh also was the liaison between the team and the coach and management. He had to negotiate any problems that came up between them.

The best way to lead is by example. "Only ask the players to do what you can do yourself. Don't expect players to do what you cannot do yourself," Marsh said. "Always give positive encouragement no matter what is happening."

In playing his position, he recommends that you always try to pass the ball as soon as you can. "That means don't hold the ball just for the sake of self-enjoyment. Get it and give it," Marsh emphasized. "You will still have opportunities for those big plays."

The best players use brilliant one-touches. "Most goals are scored with one touch of the ball, first time header or first time shot," Marsh explained. "So if there is plenty of opportunity there, then there is plenty of opportunity for brilliant one touches in other areas of the field."

During the first ten minutes of a game, the Rowdies play so that nothing is given away. "We don't overextend ourselves, especially away from home games. When the game starts we try to get the continuity going, giving everyone a touch on the ball, including the goalkeeper." The Rowdies mark their opponents tight, waiting until they have the game under control before launching an attack.

When it comes to scoring on penalty kicks, Marsh is considered one of the best in the world. A miss in Philadelphia in 1979 marred his 100 percent success record.

Before you take the penalty kick, observe the goalkeeper and see how he positions himself. Notice which side he favors. If he favors his left hand side, he may lean slightly to his right to encourage you to shoot to his left. In this situation, aim your shot to his right. Always look for clues where he plans to dive.

"Once you've decided which side you're going to take, don't change your mind," Marsh explained. "Keep yourself bent over the ball and use your instep. Aim your shot as far into the corner as you can. Give yourself some safety margin so that if you slightly miss it, the ball won't hit the post or go wide. Conserve your power when you kick it so you get the most accuracy possible."

Before Marsh takes the shot, he always pictures the whole sequence in his mind. "I picture where I am going to place the ball, where the goalkeeper will dive, and then the ball going into the back of the net," he explained. "It's as simple as that. It may not work for everybody, but it works for me."

On the night before a game, he spends about half an hour playing the game in his mind. "They're usually the same situations, the ones I'll be involved in, like goalmouth incidents, shooting, heading, penalty kicks or free kicks, and stuff like that. I have a built-in mental picture of all the positive things that can happen. I've always done it. They say people play better when they've rehearsed the game in their minds."

Since Marsh has a photographic memory, he can recall most of the facts about an opponent he needs to know to play well against him. When he rehearses the game in his mind, he imagines himself exploiting his opponent's weaknesses and overcoming his strengths. "The things you remember from past games that you've played can be of tremendous help," he said. "You think about something that happened in a game last year because it might happen again this year. Powers of recall are very important."

His mental imagery comes into play during games. When there is sufficient time, the picture of him making a perfect pass or scoring a goal will flash through his mind. Instead of the whole action sequence, he only imagines the end result, like the ball in the back of the net or his pass going right to his teammate's feet.

Rather than recommending a specific technique for those interested in mental imagery, he suggests forming a style of your own. "It's a very individual thing. Imagine the things you want, like positive situations. Always avoid negative situations. Make sure they are positive." He never allows a negative thought to enter his mind.

"I think this is fantasy, really," he said. "But if you have the skill, you can make fantasy fact. Then it really isn't fantasy."

Momentum is a key ingredient in any successful attack on goal. If the player with the ball hesitates or breaks the rhythm, the whole attack can fall apart.

Peripheral vision is essential to maintain the momentum of attack because you have to know what is going on around you to shoot or make accurate forward passes. "The ultimate quality of a player is decided on whether his peripheral vision is at a high or low standard. This is true for a forward, midfielder, and defender," Marsh said. "Once you control the ball, you should know where it is. You shouldn't have to keep looking down at it when you're dribbling."

Marsh is reknowned for his play-making ability. His talent for knowing which player to pass the ball to for setting up a goal-scoring situation has won many games for the Rowdies.

The real test of a playmaker occurs when he has two players or more open to whom he can pass the ball. Since one of the two players will be in a better position to shoot on goal or continue the momentum of the attack, the playmaker must pass to him rather than the other teammate.

"The great player will pick out eight out of ten, the average player will pick four out of ten, and the bad player one out of ten," he explained. "The determining factor is how well you read the game. In my case, my selection is just pure instinct."

One drill players and coaches can use to improve creative playmaking is play three-against-three without goals in a confined area. Restrict the number of times a player can touch the ball before passing it to two, and later to one touch. "That way they must get their head up and look around for support," Marsh said. "Otherwise, they are going to lose the ball."

Marsh is a master of ball control, being able to trap and make moves with the ball other players only dream about. "Ball control is the most important part of the game," he said. "Practice everyday, keep the ball up juggling it, kicking it against the wall. Be able to juggle it off of your shoulder, head, thigh, foot, every part of your body. Get a feel of the ball on every inch of your foot. This will not only help your ball control, but also improve your passing and shooting ability."

According to Marsh trial-and-error is a good way to improve your shooting accuracy. Find out what works for you and improve on it. Try to correct your weaknesses and turn them into strengths. Practice your shooting every day.

To keep control of the ball under pressure, maintain your balance. "If an opponent tries to shoulder you off the ball, keep your feet wide apart so you can absorb his pressure," he advised. "You also try and keep the ball on the farthest foot away from the attacker. If the opponent pressures you on your left side, keep the ball on your right foot. If he comes in from the right, keep the ball on your left foot."

Marsh enjoys practicing everyday. He also has a twenty-five-minute daily exercise routine, which may be the reason he is in better physical condition than a lot of younger players. Before he begins the exercises, he loosens up with static stretches. Then he works on his abdominal muscles with exercises like sit-ups using weights. The routine also includes one hundred push-ups. Instead of doing his routine at a specific time each day, he exercises when he feels like it.

Marsh's attitude has contributed a great deal to maintaining his superior physical fitness. "My attitude to the game is I love to win. I like to be in the best shape possible. The only way to achieve that is to train well in practice. That's why I have the urge to practice," he explained. "The only way to play is to win. So you have to train to win."

Julie Veee
San Diego Sockers

Creativity is one of the keys to being a good midfielder and Julie Veee of the San Diego Sockers is perhaps one of the most inventive midfielders in the North American Soccer League.

Born in Budapest, Hungary on February 22, 1950, Veee has always been a creative player from the time he started playing with a soccer ball at age two-and-a-half.

Veee's father worked in a factory and played on a second-division soccer team. "He really loved soccer," Veee said. "He took me to games. I learned a lot watching him play. He was a technical player, a very good player. At halftime the players taught the kids different soccer skills.

"When you grow up in that kind of background you're always around a soccer ball. In Hungary there are millions of teams, there is the first division, second division and so on. They have district division and then the factory divisions. It's up to your ability whether you're going to make it."

At age nine, Veee joined his class team and at age twelve he made his school team (the next step up).

"In the United States, there are a million and one things that can distract a kid, television, records, cars, football, basketball, baseball, you name it. In Hungary all you have is soccer so you really start falling in love with that. You live in that life," Veee said.

When he reached age fourteen, Veee was selected for the

junior team made up of the best players fourteen to eighteen years of age. Two years later he was advanced to the second team, and then to the first team. Playing with the older players helped him mature physically and technically. When he played in a couple of games for a junior team comprised of teams his own age, the training, experience, and confidence he had acquired playing with the older players made him a superior player among his peers.

At age eighteen, he was chosen to play with the Budapest Select Under-Twenty-One Team. While the team was on a tour in Italy, Veee requested political asylum and defected to the United States. Since an uncle lived in Long Beach, California, Veee moved there in 1969. Because several teams in the NASL folded that year, he was unable to find a professional team to play for. Instead he got a job and played on a semi-professional team in the Greater Los Angeles League.

In 1971 Veee went to France to play professional soccer. The Hungarian manager of a French team asked him to sign a one-season contract. Since he could not read the contract because it was in French, Veee accepted the club manager's word as true and signed the contract. At the end of the year, he spoke to them about renegotiating the terms of the contract. The club management told him that the contract was valid for four years and could not be renegotiated. Disgusted with the manager's lies and the whole situation with the French team, Veee brought his wife and daughter back to the United States.

Because the contract was legal Veee was prohibited from playing with another professional team. In 1975, FIFA ruled he could sever his contract with the French club. Then he signed a contract with the Los Angeles Aztecs and played midfield for them that season. He scored six goals and assisted on five others that year. In 1976 the San Jose Earthquakes purchased his contract. Before he broke his ankle during the eleventh game of the season, he assisted on six goals.

The Quakes traded him to Lierse in Belgium that fall where he scored eight goals playing wing. The renowned Standard Liege of Belgium acquired him and assigned him to midfield again. He scored seven goals for that team. In 1978 the San Diego Sockers purchased his contract and he has played there ever since.

When he became a United States citizen he was asked to play on the United States National Team and has played in several international games.

Every midfielder as well as every player should be able to make good passes. You should be able to pass the ball with the inside of the foot, instep, and also the outside of the foot. If an opponent is standing between you and the team-mate you want to pass to, then you want to bend the ball with a banana kick, making it curl in the shape of a banana around the opponent to your teammate.

Veee does not bend a ball with the outside of his foot the same way many other players do. "I strike the ball with the base of the little toe, from where the little toe starts to about an inch up," he said. "Just where bone sticks out a little bit, that's where I kick the ball.

"A lot of people maybe go toward the arch for a banana shot. But to get a good, big bend on the ball, a good curve, you've got to hit it like a cue ball. If you want to right angle it, you've got to hit it just a little bit. If you put too much arch on it, it won't bend that much. If you put just a little bit on it, it will curve around."

When he curls a ball with the inside of his foot, he strikes the ball with the base of his big toe, from where the big toe starts to about an inch up. If you curl the ball with the base of the big toe on your right foot, the ball will bend to the left. If you strike the ball with the base of the little toe on your right foot, the ball will curve in a banana shape to the right.

"We used to kick them from the six-yard line and also on the goal line," Veee recalled. "Then we put the ball down on the goal line about two-and-a-half yards from the goalpost and tried to bend the ball into the other side of the net. That's when you really have to put a curve on it."

Since there is no one correct way to kick a banana shot, someday someone might discover a new way to hit the ball. Veee recalls one very good player in Hungary who was able to bend the ball with the outside of his ankle. "He just

Julie Veee (22)

tapped it and would have fantastic shots," he said. "Soccer is not like football where you run a pattern and that's it. Every soccer player right now can invent something new. Of course, things like scissors kicks have already been invented, but you can always invent a little different move or turn or technique. That's what's so fantastic about the game of soccer."

Every player should learn to use both his right and left foot. Too many right-footed players waste opportunities switching the ball to their right foot to make a pass or take a shot, just as too many left-footed players waste opportunities changing the ball to the left foot instead of passing or shooting with the right foot.

While many players can kick the ball with power when shooting on goal, not all of them have pinpoint accuracy, Veee explained. When you practice shooting on goal, know where you want the ball to go. Aim shots at the upper right corner of the net, the lower left corner, left and right. Practice shooting until you can place a shot anywhere you want to with finite accuracy.

"You have to shoot and shoot constantly, volley the ball, half volley. Shoot from every position and distance around the goal," Veee said. "Because you seldom hit a still ball in a game, push the ball ahead or right or left, and then shoot. You always want to practice shooting a moving ball, just like in a game."

In launching an attack, midfielders should keep the ball in the part of the field where you are the strongest and your opponents are their weakest. "Play the ball wherever you have the advantage," Veee said. "You can't say you always do this, keep it wide outside, or do that, keep it in the middle of the field. If you have a couple of good wingers, then you just give them the ball and let them cross it. But if you have a couple of good players up front, play 1-2 (wall pass) with them. It's optional, it's up to the players you play with and the situation. You can't put a finger on that."

While long passes are difficult to disguise, you can disguise short passes. If you take a big swing at the ball, everybody will think you are going to make a long pass and move in that direction. Then just tap the ball with your ankle to the left or right to a teammate. Another passing disguise is to go through the motions of passing to the left and pass it to the right. You can also call out or point to a teammate and then pass the ball in the opposite direction. If your opponents are drawn in the direction you want to go, then your disguise is not successful.

"You can disguise a pass in a million ways," he said. "It's all up to each individual and what they like to do."

The more ball control midfielders have, the better they can create opportunities for the team to score. If you dribble down field and make a long pass, your forward only has a fifty-fifty chance of getting the ball.

"Generally speaking, the team that controls the ball is going to win the game because they create more chances to score," Veee explained.

Peripheral vision is essential for good ball control and playing well. If you cannot control the ball unless you look at it, the only area you can see is within two-three yards of the ball. Your limited perspective may cause you to make only two-three yard passes and passes to the other team. When you can look up and run with the ball at the same time, you see the players around you, who is open for a pass, and where the scoring opportunities are. The opposing defenders do not know what you are going to do next because you have multiple passing choices. If you look down at the ball, your only passing choice is whoever comes into view.

Veee can run almost as fast with the ball as without it. "I speed but I don't kick the ball away from me. If you have control of the ball skill-wise and can run at the same time, if a defender tries to stick his foot in there, there's no way he can take it away from you because you always have that little extra quickness," he said.

To develop better control of the ball when dribbling through traffic, dribble with the ball between your feet up and down the field. "You tap it with one touch of the inside of the right foot, then one touch with the inside of the left foot. Do it as fast as possible up and down the field. After a while you don't even think about it, it just comes naturally," Veee said. "Keep your upper body over the ball. So when somebody comes in to attack, keep the ball between your feet. If he comes around the right side, keep your body over the ball and push it to the left side, so the ball is too far away for the defender to tackle." If the defender hits you while trying to tackle the ball, the referee should call a foul.

When you want to speed-dribble up field and keep the ball away from anyone chasing you, keep the ball on the outside of your feet. If an opponent comes at you from the left side, dribble with the outside of your right foot. If he comes at you from the right, speed dribble with the outside of the left foot. The ability to dribble with either foot is most important.

Because Veee often moves forward from the midfield into the forward line when his team attacks, he is called an attacking midfielder. He is most creative in setting up goal-scoring situations for his teammates and also scoring goals himself. In 1978 he scored seven goals and had thirteen assists, and ten goals and eight assists in 1979.

When an attacking midfielder dribbles the ball forward, you want to pass your opponent midfielder because then you have automatically created a two-on-one situation with one of your forwards. Because you are now unmarked with the ball in the penalty area, one of the defenders must leave the forward he has been marking and attack you. This leaves your teammate open for a pass. If you pass the ball to him, run forward while the defender turns to attack the forward, your teammate can pass the ball back to you in a quick wall pass.

"Sometimes when you're running down the right side, you'll draw two defenders into attacking you. They're making a big mistake because now two of your forwards are open for a pass. That's why you have to keep your head up, to see who's open and what's going on around you. You get a wall pass or lay it off and let the guy take it from there," Veee explained. "Sometimes defenders will hold on to the forwards they're marking so when the forwards spread out when you bring the ball up, the defenders stay right with them. Everybody opens up like an umbrella. Just keep going forward with the ball until someone attacks you. If no one does, then you have a shot going from the eighteen-yard line or closer."

While few set plays are used in soccer, one play that Veee and his teammates use is called "leave it." "You're running at full speed with the ball at the goal and a defender comes in. You make a fake to right or left, and step on the ball so it stays dead. You make the run to the left or right and ninety-nine percent of the time the defender will follow you for a second," he said. "When you leave the ball the guy five to eight yards behind you runs up and shoots it. Everything is full speed but the ball must stay in one place."

Communication is absolutely essential in a set play. This play will only work if you and your teammates have practiced leaving the ball behind until everyone knows instinctively what you are going to do or your teammate tells you "leave it." Another variation of this play is when you pass the ball back five yards with your heel to the teammate behind you to shoot.

Attacking midfielders should always be alert to opportunities to make a through pass, passing the ball just behind the defense for a forward to run onto and shoot. "The forward creates the opportunity for a through pass, not the midfielder," Veee said. "If the forward is pressed against the defense, if he can't go forward because he'll be offsides, you have to have the ability to see he's ready to make a great move, and then pass the ball into open space in front of him. You can't just kick the ball and then hope somebody runs into it. Sometimes the forward is already running toward the defense and all you have to do is follow it up with a pass behind the defenders for him to run onto and shoot."

If a player wants to become really good, he should play a lot of games, especially games like five-aside. "Play with the ball as much as possible," Veee emphasized. "After your team practice, go home and play some more. Strengthen the skills you're good at and improve the skills you're not good at. Always have fun."

Part Three

The Defenders

Carlos Alberto
New York Cosmos

One of the greatest international defensive players in soccer is Carlos Alberto, sweeper for the New York Cosmos. He has won almost every honor in soccer and throughout his career has played with and against the best players in the world, including the great Pele who was his teammate with the Cosmos and with Santos of Brazil.

With fourteen years of experience, Alberto is famous for his ability to anticipate the next moves of his opponents and thus is almost unbeatable as a defender.

He was born July 17, 1944 in Rio de Janeiro and, like most Brazilian players, Alberto started playing with a soccer ball almost on the day that he could walk. He and his friends played soccer everywhere they could, though there were no organized youth leagues.

"In Brazil, all kids are basically born already liking the game of soccer. By having a ball with you all the time, your interest automatically expands. Because soccer is the principal sport for the tiny tots all the way to the adults, soccer is a way of life in Brazil," Alberto said.

"Every kid in Brazil dreams of becoming a professional soccer player. Every kid has a soccer hero. Mine was Milton Santos, the best defensive soccer player I have ever seen play. He was the mirror for me. I tried to play just like him."

Alberto started out playing goalkeeper but soon moved to right fullback. Because of his athletic abilities and talents, his soccer skills and understanding of the game, he was selected at age fourteen for the youth team of the world renowned Fluminense of Rio. During the next three years, he trained and played under top Brazilian youth coaches in the club's juvenile program designed for developing young players for the club's first team.

At age seventeen, Alberto signed a professional contract with Fluminense and played right fullback on the first team until 1966 when Santos purchased his contract. In 1975 Fluminense bought his contract back. After thirteen years playing right fullback, he changed to centerback under the Brazilian sweeper system of two centerbacks. He led Fluminense to two Rio championships. The following season he played for Flamengo of Rio de Janeiro.

He also played on the Brazilian National Team seventy-three times and captained the team that won the 1970 World Cup.

On loan from Flamengo of Rio de Janeiro for the last four games in the Cosmos 1977 season, Alberto played so well that the Cosmos purchased his contract and he has played for New York ever since. Along with the numerous honors and awards he received in 1978 and 1979, he was voted on the North American Soccer League All-Star first team and the Professional Soccer Reporters Association All-Star first team twice in a row.

Alberto's style of playing sweeper with the New York Cosmos is not the same style he played for Fluminense and Santos. In New York he is the last man in the defense, playing behind the right, center, and left fullbacks.

"The difference between the two styles is that in Brazil, the sweeper position does not exist, compared to Europe, here, and other countries," Alberto explained. "In Europe the sweeper is known as 'libero,' meaning 'free' in Italian. He is free to move around. I didn't start playing sweeper until I started playing with the Cosmos."

In Brazil, he was one of two centerbacks in a four-man defense. The two centerbacks positioned themselves in the middle with the right and left fullbacks on either side. If an opposing winger dribbles the ball down the left side, the left

Carlos Alberto (5)

fullback would take him on. The left centerback would mark the opposing center forward while the right centerback would drop back to cover in the event the winger beat the left fullback and attacked the goal. The right centerback also has to cover the left centerback in case the winger passes the ball to the center forward who beats the left centerback and attacks the goal.

If the winger beats the left fullback and the left centerback is closer to him than the right centerback, then the left centerback will take on the winger. At the same time, the right centerback picks up the center forward.

If the opposing team attacks with two wingers and two forwards in the center, each centerback has a forward to mark. If an opposing winger dribbles down the left side, the left fullback takes him on and the left centerback stays with his forward. The right centerback drops back to cover, but he also must keep track of the forward he has been marking, in case the winger crosses the ball into the middle of the field.

In that situation, the centerback must get back to his man right away.

If the right fullback has come in toward the center of the field, he can also help the right centerback. Because soccer is a fluid game without rigid formations, every situation is different. Many players rely on experience and their ability to read the game to know what to do in different situations.

In playing sweeper for the Cosmos, Alberto usually does not have any specific man to mark. He is free to stay behind the three fullbacks, covering each of them, and picking up any opponent who breaks through. Since he is further back than the others, he can see more of what is happening on the field and can help direct the fullbacks into better positions and warn them if an opponent is about to take advantage of them, like a winger trying to get behind an outside fullback.

"Because the sweeper is the last man of the defense, you need experience," Alberto said. "You get more experience every game you play. Learn from your mistakes, learn from players you play with and against, always try to improve yourself."

Some teams play with the sweeper (stopper) in front of the three fullbacks. Most teams use a sweeper rather than a stopper for a strong defense.

Alberto brought innovation into Brazilian soccer when he started launching counterattacks from the back, going forward with the ball and attacking the opponents' goal. "When your team has the ball and goes forward, the sweeper goes too. The sweeper stays behind only when the other team goes forward," he said. "But you do not go all the way forward all the time because you want to surprise the other team when you go up front with your own forwards and attack their goal."

Unlike other sweepers, Alberto almost never attacks straight up the middle. "I attack up the right side or left side because there are usually more players in the middle of the field," he said. "If there are a lot of players on the left side, I go up on the right side. If the other team has a lot of players on the right side, I run up the left side. I go up the side where there are the fewest players because that gives me more open space to help my teammates."

He starts the attack by passing to a midfielder. If Alberto has the opportunity to go forward, he runs up the wing and the midfielder passes the ball back to him in a wall pass. If no defender challenges Alberto, he continues dribbling up the wing. If an opponent challenges him, Alberto will play wall passes up the wing until he gets into a position to cross the ball on the ground to his forwards in front of the opponents' goal.

"Sometimes I shoot from the outside, but if I am outside the eighteen-yard box, I prefer to make the cross to a teammate who is in a better position to take the shot on goal," Alberto explained. "When I am close in the penalty area, then I take a quick shot with the ball."

When you go all the way up the right or left wing, you free your winger to go inside and join the other forwards in attacking the opponents' goal. If the defender who has been marking the winger now challenges you, your winger may now be unmarked and in a goal-scoring position and you can pass him the ball. If none of the defenders take you on, you can come inside yourself or get into an even better position to make the cross. When you go all the way up front in the attack, you give your forwards a numerical advantage, except when an opposing winger or forward comes up with you and tries to mark you tight.

When you start the attack from the back and go forward, one of your midfielders will drop back and cover for you while you are up front. If no one comes back while you are forward, then your defense is a man short, should the other team gain possession of the ball and attack. If your opponents get the ball while you are up front, you must drop back into the midfield and cover for the midfielder who is covering for you. As soon as the opportunity arises, the midfielder comes forward into the midfield and you go back into your regular sweeper position, Alberto explained.

"If you don't feel the time is right to go forward, then stay in back," he advised. "You only go in the attack when the opportunity looks right for you. Your experience tells you when the situation is right to go forward and when to stay back."

Alberto takes a very serious approach toward soccer and

practice. During the regular practice sessions with the team coach, Alberto does everything the other players do; sprints, passing and shooting drills, offense and defense. When practice is over he does his own practice routine which he has developed over the years.

"It's a combination of several kinds of exercises including running and kicking the ball. Every day I work hard on the field," Alberto said. "I practice even more by myself than I do with the coach. I know just what I have to do."

Alberto also practices thirty to forty penalty kicks every day with a goalkeeper. "We need a lot of exercises because in a game, it is very easy to score," he said. "I think you need to be calm. If you stay calm, you improve your chances for scoring a goal. If you get nervous, you can't kick the ball well. So calm yourself before you take a penalty kick."

When you are about to take the penalty kick, you should keep your head up. Do not look down at the ball. If you watch the goalkeeper, you can see which way he moves. If you watch the ball, you see the ball but you cannot see what the goalkeeper is doing. Striking the ball properly without looking at it requires lots of practice.

Know which side you want to kick the ball before you go to take the kick. You should keep your head up and watch for any last-minute sign that will help improve your chances of scoring, you will see the opportunity and take advantage of it. If you see the goalkeeper leaning too far left you can shoot the ball to the right and score. If he shifts his balance just before you shoot, you can change the side at which you will shoot. After you kick the ball, follow up on it in the event it bounces off the goalkeeper, giving you another chance to score.

Penalty kicks should be hard, powerful shots just inside the goalpost. Instead of shooting high or low, hit the ball in about knee high, making it most difficult for the goalkeeper to save.

"For me soccer is very serious," Alberto said. "A player has to think seriously in respect to playing soccer. Soccer is not a joking matter. Have fun and enjoy playing soccer, but also concentrate with a serious attitude on the game."

Because Americans have taken a serious attitude toward the development of soccer in the United States, he foresees a great future in American soccer. He believes the organization of soccer here provides a sound base for growth in the game, possibly unequalled anywhere, including Brazil.

"American players are more athletic than Brazilians, based on their physical size, but they lack the technical development, the ball skills Brazilians learn almost from the day they're born," Alberto said. "With the proper coaching, Americans can become technically skilled on a world class level."

The fact that thousands of American youth players go to soccer camps every summer proves the seriousness of American interest in the game. He would like to see more Americans attend soccer camps because this is where they will receive the coaching they need. Of course, not every soccer camp has top coaches, which is why they should be checked out before any tuition is paid.

While professional soccer clubs in the United States do not now have development programs for fourteen to eighteen year olds, Alberto looks forward to when they do, like the Fluminense program he went through.

"Most professional soccer teams throughout the world have their own youth leagues where young players develop," he said. "Generally, these are the players who advance into the professional ranks at age eighteen to nineteen years old." (In Europe many professional soccer clubs have youth leagues for players as young as six-years old.)

A professional club's youth league is usually divided into various age groups, like under sixteens. Players are selected for a local club team in their age group and coached by a licensed coach assigned by the club. They play against other club teams in their age group and often play almost all year. As the players progress and grow older, the best players from an age group are brought up into the club teams at the next higher level in the program.

When the best players in the club's youth development program reach age sixteen, they are advanced into the reserve team and become apprentice professionals. In some countries, players do not enter a reserve team until they are eighteen. The reserve team is one level below the first team, which is the club's top team competing against other professional teams in the league.

Players in the reserve team work on developing their physical abilities and talents, skills and techniques, and expanding their knowledge of the game, tactics, and learning finer points of the game. They practice and play every day under a professional coach. Some clubs have their reserve teams practice right alongside or with their first team players, where the reserve players gain individual coaching from the seasoned professional players. The reserve team scrimmages the first team and plays against other reserve teams in the league. Those who make it through the reserve team sign professional contracts and are brought up to the first team.

Rhythm is most important in playing soccer. If a player has rhythm in his style of play, he is more relaxed in the game, is better able to flow with the pulse of the game, and enjoys better ball control skills. Alberto believes the Brazilians' rhythm definitely helped them win three World Cups.

"You must have concentration in the game," Alberto advised. "Have fun and enjoy yourself when you play, but have a serious attitude, always work to improve yourself and play your best."

Franz Beckenbauer
New York Cosmos

Known to millions around the world as Der Kaiser, Franz Beckenbauer is probably the best known and respected international soccer hero playing the game today. During his thirteen years with Bayern Munich of the West German Bundesliga, Beckenbauer revolutionized the sweeper position which changed the whole game of soccer.

In the late 1960's when he played with the elite Bayern Munich of the West German Bundesliga, Franz Beckenbauer changed the defensive role of the sweeper to make him an extra man on offense.

"The sweeper is the most creative position on the field. You're the only man on the field who is free. You can run over the whole field and nobody is marking you," Beckenbauer explained. "You have to do everything. You have to organize the defense by shouting advice, directions, and encouragement to your defenders. When you get the ball, you have to start the attack, support your midfielders, and when it is possible, go forward with your teammates and score. The sweeper has to do everything that is possible in a soccer game."

The basic position of the sweeper is behind the fullbacks. If an opponent gets past one of them, the sweeper has to cover and take the opponent on. This means you have to tackle well. To launch an attack when you have the ball requires that you be able to pass well and possess good ball control. If you go forward into the attack, you must be able to dribble and shoot well. Because the sweeper does play the entire field, you should have the ability to read the game, comprehend the flow of the game and anticipate what will happen next.

"You must know your teammates, what their strengths and weaknesses are," Beckenbauer said. "If your right back is not doing well against the opposing left winger, you will have to watch them and perhaps give your fullback a little more support than the other defenders. If the left winger gets past him, you have to pick him up and prevent him from scoring a goal," he said. "You also have to support everyone else in the defense. You are the last man in the defense."

Beckenbauer did not play defender until age seventeen. Before then he always played center forward. Born on September 11, 1945, in Munich, West Germany, he grew up in the era of reconstruction after World War II. Because money was scarce, he and his friends could not afford to buy a soccer ball. To earn the price of a ball, they collected and sold old newspapers and iron. After five months they were able to buy a ball.

"It belonged to all of us," Beckenbauer recalled. "We played every day, mornings, and after school. I was born in a house next to a soccer field so I only had to cross the street and I was on the field."

He did not play on an organized team until age ten which was the minimum age at that time. When he turned thirteen he joined Bayern Munich's youth league where he advanced through the various levels, playing on the league's best teams for his age group.

During the 1950s Bayern Munich and the other first division soccer clubs were still semi-professional. The players worked at their jobs in the mornings and played soccer in the afternoons. The teams turned professional in the 1960s and have since become among the greatest clubs in the world.

Around age sixteen Beckenbauer ran into some problems with his soccer coach. "I was emotional, I was against everything. I played on Bayern Munich's first youth team. The coach said to me, 'If you don't change your mind, your life, then you'll play in the second team.' I couldn't change then and he put me on the second team," Beckenbauer said. "I was of course disappointed, upset, but it was very helpful for me. Then the next year he asked me, 'You would like to start again in the first team?' I had matured during that year and told him so. He said, 'Now you are all right,' and put me on the first team."

Until he turned seventeen he always played center forward, scoring many goals. Although the coach had put Beckenbauer back on the first team, he did not always play him as the center forward. Instead he sometimes put Beckenbauer in at right or left wing which was not his best position. This was the year Beckenbauer needed to excel because at the end of the season, Bayern Munich would decide which players would continue playing on an amateur basis and which ones would sign professional contracts.

During an exhibition match the team's centerback was injured and had to be taken out of the game, making the team play one man short. "At that time there were no substitutions allowed. We had to play with ten men," Beckenbauer recalled. "So the coach said to me, 'You go back and play centerback the rest of the game.' From that moment on, I always played centerback and later sweeper." Bayern Munich then signed Beckenbauer to a professional contract.

While none of the World Cup contenders used a sweeper in the 1962 competition, many of the top European teams implemented the position before the 1966 World Cup. In those years the sweeper defended and organized the defense but never attacked.

While he was still a center forward, Beckenbauer had watched and studied Facchetti, who played left fullback for then famous Inter Milan of Italy. When Beckenbauer became a sweeper, he developed his own style of attack, charging up the middle into the midfield to support the forwards and later joining the forwards in attacking the opponents' goal. Not limited to running up the middle, he sometimes went up the wing into the opponents' penalty area to cross the ball to the center forward or to score the goal himself.

"I scored a lot of goals because everybody was surprised,"

Beckenbauer explained. "I went to the midfield, I went forward, this was a new style of soccer." Within two years almost every sweeper followed suit.

Selected for the West German National Team, he played in the 1966 and 1970 World Cup finals. In 1974 Beckenbauer captained the team which won the cup from the Dutch. During his thirteen seasons with Bayern Munich, the club won three Bundesliga championships, three European Cups, four German Cups, and one Cup Winners Cup. He was named European Footballer of the Year in 1972 and 1976, and German Footballer of the Year in 1966, 1968, 1974, and 1976. On May 25, 1977 he joined the New York Cosmos and moved up to the position of midfielder. He has played midfield and sweeper ever since.

Physical fitness is a definite requirement of every sweeper. "Because you have to go forward, support the midfielders and forwards, you have to run a lot during the game," Beckenbauer said. "You also have to have very good technique and skills. You must be able to make quick short passes as well as long accurate passes to midfielders and forwards. You must be able to do everything on the field."

A modest man who enjoys helping young players, Beckenbauer has a deep desire to see soccer become as great in the United States as it is around the rest of the world.

"It is very important for a soccer player, especially a youth, to watch soccer games. Watch the great players, like Carlos Alberto," he said. "You can learn a lot from watching. Then afterward try to copy what a player did. Try to reach the same level."

During his youth, Beckenbauer and his friends went to the city stadium and watched a professional game almost every Sunday.

"I enjoyed going to the games and watching the players," he recalled. "I watched how they move, how they stop the ball, pass, and shoot. There are so many different ways to handle a ball you don't see them all in just a few games. You get the feeling how the game is going on."

Also watch the teamwork on the field, how the defense works together, how the forwards coordinate their attack,

Franz Beckenbauer (6)

how the midfielders organize their team's play and set the tempo of the game, and how the goalkeeper works with his defenders. See how quickly they can counterattack and how well they organize themselves on defense and offense. Note each team's strengths and weaknesses, and then do the same for individual players. Learn what will help you improve yourself and your game, and also what weaknesses and mistakes to avoid.

"I try to pick up the good things," Beckenbauer said. "Sometimes they play a very good winger game. Everyone should watch how he plays. In today's game, the defender has to dribble exactly the same as a winger, he must be fast like a winger, so it is good to pick up the best of each player, regardless of what position he plays."

After the game, he and his friends went home and then to the nearby soccer field where they replayed the game they had just seen. "We were all the time a group of six to ten kids," Beckenbauer said. "Each of us pretended to be one of the players we had watched at the game. We tried to do everything they had done, to make the same moves, to dribble, pass, tackle, and shoot like they did. It was a lot of fun."

When you imagine yourself playing like a player you watched in a game, try to feel the game the way he did. Adopt his style and characteristics. If you are the midfielder, make your passes crisp and set up plays for your forwards. If you are the forward or winger, beat the defender with the fakes and moves you saw in the game. Curl the ball around the goalkeeper into the back of the net. If you are a goalkeeper, position yourself like the goalkeeper you saw and use his style in making the saves. If you are a fullback or sweeper, force the forwards to do what you want them to, use the skills and techniques you observed in the game.

"Find a player you like, then try to do everything he does," he said. "Watch everything he does, then imitate him in every detail. This is very important for a youth player. Try to reach his level, always try to improve, but always have fun and enjoy yourself."

Before going to bed at night, Beckenbauer replayed various portions of the game in his mind. If he had seen a brilliant goal scored, he imagined himself scoring the goal. Playing the game in his mind was a fun experience.

Beckenbauer still watches games and learns from them. "If I see a great game, I pick up things because sometimes you forget little things. It motivates me a little bit," he said. "You never stop learning. Everybody has to improve a little bit, your left leg, or the free kick or corner kick, whatever it might be. This is why we have practice every day."

While you can learn more about the game from watching soccer on television, you will gain more in seeing a professional game in a stadium. "When you go to the stadium, you get more of the atmosphere and emotion of the game," he explained. "You also have a much better view in the stadium because the TV only shows the part where the ball is. Watch the movement of the whole team."

If the left winger has the ball, then see what the right full-back is doing. Observe what the other forwards on the attacking team are doing. See what the defense is doing. Watch the total movement on the field.

Since the sweeper is the last man in the defense, you have to know how your team and the opponents are moving during the game. On defense you have to read the game well to best position yourself and your defenders. On offense you have to understand the movement of the game to launch an attack with the best chance of scoring a goal.

On the field Beckenbauer constantly looks to see what is happening around him. His head never seems to stop turning from one side to the other. Because he sees everything that goes on, he can better anticipate what will happen next, and do whatever is best to prevent or support it.

Another of Beckenbauer's characteristics is his famed ability to pass, shoot, and control the ball with the outside of his feet. In the Munich youth league, at least one coach tried to dissuade him from using the outside of his feet because no one playing in Germany used the outside of his feet at that time.

"Maybe the reason I like to play the ball with the outside of the foot is that I walked pigeon toed until I was about six or seven years old," he said. "So it was easy for me, a natural way to play with the outside of the foot. Always be flexible, try doing different things different ways."

Another characteristic of his style is his continuous movement. He almost never stands still during the game, but always moves around a little even when the ball is at the other end of the field.

"When the ball is coming at you, you have to look around and see where your free players are. Before you stop the ball, you have to know where you are going to pass it," he advised. "That is very important. If you wait to look around until after you get the ball, you may lose it. That's the difference between a good player and one who isn't."

You also have to learn to stay cool in pressured situations, like when the ball is passed to you and two opponents come in to tackle you. "The better your technique, the better you can play under pressure. Don't get nervous, keep cool," Beckenbauer explained. "You must have confidence on the field. The more you improve your technique and skills, the more confidence you will have."

Before a game relax yourself. Take deep breaths and tell yourself to relax, Beckenbauer said. After a while any nervousness you may have had will vanish. Clear everything out of your mind except the game. Concentrate only on the game until the referee blows his whistle ending the match.

If you are playing against an equal or superior team, you usually find it easier to concentrate on the game because you are more stimulated than when playing a weak team. You have to concentrate on playing well or the other team will score. The better you can focus your concentration on the game and maintain it, the more confidence you will have during the match. If you find your mind is wandering, pay attention to the movement of the game. Try to anticipate what may happen next.

Attitude is most important in becoming a good soccer player. "If you go into a game with the right attitude, that you are going to give 100 percent, then you will have a good game," Beckenbauer emphasized. "On the other hand, if you go to the game with a lousy attitude, then it is impossible for you to play a good game. You must have the right attitude and give 100 percent in everything you do."

You also have to give 100 percent in every practice session as well as in every game. Always do your best to improve, develop your skills and technique, become the best player you possibly can. To be a top player, you must also be physically fit. Train well and prepare your body to play your best for the entire 90 minutes of the game. Eat the right food, avoid drugs, tobacco, and alcohol.

Learn to play all the positions. Beckenbauer played every position on the field and also spent a little time in goal. Wait until you are a teenager before you specialize in one position.

"You have to love the sport, otherwise forget it. If your parents tell you that you have to play tennis, but you don't like it, then you will never reach a high level in the game. But if you would rather play tennis than soccer, play tennis. If you love soccer, then play soccer," he advised.

"Now with my seventeenth season as a professional soccer player, I still love the game," Beckenbauer said. "I am happy when I have the ball, to win games, to play soccer with my teammates."

Mike Connell
Tampa Bay Rowdies

One of the youngest and most agile sweepers in the NASL is 23-year-old Mike Connell of the Tampa Bay Rowdies. Quick into the tackle and quick to recover, he possesses the keen ability to read the game well, often stopping the opponents' attack before it has begun. Born in Johannesburg, South Africa on November 1, 1956, he became a professional soccer player at age 17 in South Africa and has played with the Rowdies since 1975.

He began playing soccer at the age of seven with his brother James. They received a lot of encouragement from their father who played amateur soccer. "He never pushed us into anything. He let us do what we wanted and go the way we wanted to go, within reason of course," Mike recalled. "He kicked the ball with us in the street and often watched us play, just to keep our interest high."

His father's encouragement helped Mike feel more confident. "You do things you wouldn't be able to do unless somebody told you that you were capable of doing them," he explained. "I think in that way even if you do have bad games or your team loses a lot, you should have somebody there to tell you that it's not a bad thing to have something like that happen."

Mike's whole family encouraged his brother and him, often attending their games and cheering them on. His brother went on to play professional soccer, but quit after a couple of seasons.

Mike did not start out playing defense. He played center forward on every team from age seven until he was sixteen. His youth teams were all part of the Johannesburg Ranger professional soccer club's program.

"I made a lot of goals," he said. "I always made the regional and state teams." He captained his state teams and later the National Under-16 Team.

When a better goal-scorer joined his under-16 team, Connell moved back to midfield. He continued playing midfield when he advanced to the Ranger's first team. Because his father wanted him to wait until he was older before signing a professional contract, Connell played with the Rangers on an amateur basis. He was only sixteen years old.

That same year he was invited to train with the under-19 youth team of the Arsenal Football Club in England. Since such an invitation was the dream come true for every young South African player, he eagerly accepted the invitation to be coached and play in one of Britain's top first division soccer clubs.

"I learned a lot about the game and gained a lot of experience in England," Connell recalled. "It helped me do things with a little bit more finesse than before. When you become professional, you see things differently, and you learn to take responsibility."

Because he could not obtain a working visa after six months in England, he returned to Johannesburg where he again played for the Rangers and also finished high school.

When then-Rowdies coach Eddie Firmani spotted Connell playing in a Ranger game in November, 1974, he invited him to come to Tampa Bay and play for the Rowdies. After signing a professional player's contract with Firmani, he came to Florida for the 1975 season. Connell missed the 1976 NASL season because he had to complete his compulsory one-year service in the South African Army. He returned to the Rowdies for the 1977 season and has played for Tampa Bay ever since.

Coach Firmani switched him from the midfield to playing sweeper and centerback. In playing defense, his style of play is more skillful than physical. "I'm aggressive, but I'm not aggressive to the point of blatant fouls," Connell said.

His ability to tackle well is a definite asset in his game. "Most of the tackles I do are standing up, not slide tackles. I wait until the forward loses control of the ball and then I just take a step forward and try to get my foot in there at the same time he's coming forward."

Connell rarely slide tackles because if you miss tackling the ball away from your opponent, you may not get the chance for another tackle. "When you go down in a slide tackle, you're left on your backside," he said. "You've given all the advantage to the other player because, if you miss, you have to get up and get after him. Whereas, if you tackle him standing up and don't get the ball, you're still on your feet. So you can quickly recover and tackle him again."

Before you go in for a tackle, you should know whether there is another defender supporting you. If a teammate is behind you and you miss a tackle, he can take over while you recover. If no one is supporting you, you should use some caution in tackling your opponent. Otherwise, if you miss, he might take a quick shot on goal or pass the ball to someone who is in a position to score.

You also should know where your opponent's teammates are before tackling him. If he has no one to pass to, he may be under pressure to try and run at the goal for a shot. The pressure may cause him to make an error, giving you a better opportunity to tackle the ball away.

If you know where his teammates are, you will be better able to know where he may want to pass the ball. When you see him bring his foot back to kick the ball, you have a better chance to block the pass.

Sometimes when a winger is speed dribbling down the touchline, it is better just to run beside him.

"By running alongside him, keeping goalside of him, he can't cross the ball and he can't come inside for a shot on goal," Connell explained. "He (the dribbler) keeps running down the touchline, waiting for you to try and tackle. You're running alongside, waiting for him to make a mistake so you can get a tackle in. If nothing happens, he might run himself

Mike Connell

right into the corner. This gives you the advantage because he has to stop, turn around, and try to do something, whereas you can just put a foot in there."

A forward with the ball who breaks through down the center of the field is a more dangerous opponent than a winger. If you miss a tackle out wide on the wing, the winger still has to cross the ball to the center or run inside to take a shot.

"If I'm one on one with a center forward, I'll jockey him until I can get some support. Then I'll go into a tackle. If I miss the tackle my teammate will get the second bite at it," Connell said. "Or I will close him down on one side, maybe go to his right so that he's forced to go to his left, and thereby go away from the danger area. You might even force him to dribble out to his left wing."

If Connell is playing sweeper and an opposing center forward beats his centerback, Connell makes sure he keeps his body between the goal and the ball. "Then I have the advantage. At all times I'm watching the ball, seeing what the opponent is going to do. If the ball does roll a couple of inches away from his foot, then I can get a tackle in."

In closing the forward down, you do not want to get too close because that would make it easier for him to get around you. If you stay too far away, then he has a chance to pass the ball or take a shot on goal.

"With me I'm six feet tall," he said. "It's really difficult for me to get close to somebody, and if I'm beaten, to stop, turn, and get after him. So I leave myself about two yards because I'm quick enough to get into a tackle from that distance and also quick enough to stop him from doing what he wants."

If a forward chips the ball over the centerback's head, the sweeper runs to the ball and either passes it back to the goalkeeper or forward to a midfielder. How well the sweeper handles the chipped ball depends on how well he is positioned. If he is out of position or not totally aware of everything happening on the field, he could be in real trouble.

"A sweeper always has to be aware of where the ball is and where all the opposing forwards as well as his own teammates are," Connell emphasized. "Unless he knows where all the players are, he cannot properly position himself."

Proper positioning is of vital importance in defending against a two-on-one situation. If the opposing center forward brings the ball down the center of the field and his right wing runs down the side, and you are the only defender between them and the goal, jockey the center forward, try to force him wide. It is to your advantage when he passes the ball out to the wing, because it is more difficult to score from the outside than from the center of the field.

"It is important for you to try to let the winger keep the ball as long as possible, hopefully, then you can get some support from other defenders," Connell advised. "Should you not get support, jockey between the two players, slowly positioning yourself closer to the winger who at the 35-yard line should have started angling into the middle of the park. Stay in the jockey position right to about the 18-yard line.

This is important as there is little space now between the goalkeeper and your position on the 18-yard line. Should the winger pass the ball past you, then the keeper might have a chance of challenging the center forward. It is also very important not to sell yourself, do not make a wild tackle and get beat."

At the 18-yard line, the winger now has three options, to dribble, pass, or shoot. This is when your composure and coolness come into the game. Cut off the winger's passing option by positioning yourself between the winger and the center forward. If the winger wants to pass now, he has to make a forward pass toward the goalkeeper for his center forward to run onto. If the winger does that, the goalkeeper will hopefully come out and get the ball before the center forward. If the winger tries to beat you, you can tackle him and get the ball. If he does not try that, his only remaining option is to take a shot.

If the center forward has the ball in the center of the field, imagine there is a spot exactly in the middle between the two goalposts. Then draw an imaginary line from the spot to the ball and position yourself within three feet of either side of that line. When the opponent dribbles the ball, keep that imaginary line drawn to the ball and position yourself accordingly. If the ball is passed out to your left side, imagine a line drawn from the left goalpost to the ball and re-position yourself.

"You want to be able to cover anything that gets past your fellow defenders," Connell said, "because you're the last man between the forward and your goalkeeper. If you're in good position, you don't have to make desperate tackles or try to sprint ten yards in two seconds. Good positioning also helps you to intercept balls that have been knocked over any of your defenders' heads. Good positioning just makes your job a little bit easier."

According to Connell the best way to master the imaginary line concept is to use it during practices. Have a teammate dribble a ball down the left side of the field. Draw your imaginary line from the left goalpost or cone to the ball and position yourself three feet or less on either side of the line. When your teammate dribbles to the right or left, adjust your imaginary line and re-position yourself so you are always in line with the ball. Then have him dribble to the center of the field so that you have to change your imaginary line to the spot between the goalposts. Continue practicing until proper positioning becomes a habit.

If you do not know where you are in relation to the goal, you may go too far to the right or left and present the forward with a perfect opportunity to shoot the ball into the back of the net.

When you practice, always try to improve and learn something new. "That's the only way you'll become a better player," he said.

The sweeper must do everything he can to prevent the winger from coming inside or passing the ball. If the winger does pass the ball to either of his forwards running unmarked in the penalty area defended by only the goalkeeper, the opponents are almost assured of scoring a goal.

"If the winger starts to pass the ball, all I can do is make a desperate tackle before he gets a shot off," he said.

During the game Connell has one constant thought running through his mind. "I don't want any goals scored against me. If fifteen minutes go by without a goal being scored, then I'm looking forward to the next fifteen minutes. I'm always putting pressure on myself so no goals are scored," he explained. "I'm always helping other players around me, talking to them, trying to lift them up a little bit. If I make a mistake and they score, that really puts that much more pressure on the players. So I always try and make sure that the player I am marking does not score and then I help the other players stop their opponents from scoring. My teammates help me too."

He also praises his teammates for good tackles, controlling their opponents, and general good play. By talking to everyone around him, he helps boost their morale, keep their interest peaked, and be totally involved in the game. When he plays sweeper, he also advises players where to position themselves.

During the first ten to fifteen minutes of the first half, he concentrates on the opposing center forward's style of play. "You watch his moves and tactics so you can counterbalance. If yours do not work successfully, then you change them. If you have to, you keep changing them until you find what works in your favor," he advised.

If your opponent changes his tactics later on, like at the beginning of the second half, you adjust your style to counterbalance his.

Each game is a learning experience. If you are alert, you can pick up little things about your opponent, his style and moves, strengths, and weaknesses, which will help you play an even better game the next time you play against him.

Being a professional, Connell always plays to win, and winning gives him a great deal of satisfaction. If his team does lose, he can still gain satisfaction, if he has played well and learned something. "Losing is not as satisfying as winning," he observed, "but if you have learned something, then you will play a better game next time."

If a forward scored a goal because he pressured you into an unexpected mistake, remember what he did so you will not permit it to ever happen again.

In the locker room before each game, Connell likes to psyche himself up. "I like to talk to my teammates about the game, certain players, I shout and get really totally involved. I like to try and pep the players up, 'Come on, let's do it for the fans' or 'we really have to win this game.' I really get involved because it psyches me up for the game," he explained. "I've found that if I don't do that, if I just go about getting dressed, keeping quiet, I'm not really geared up for the game. So I like to be about, talking and shouting to other players."

Because centerback and sweeper are pressure positions, you should not play them unless you really enjoy it. "To play sweeper, you have to be prepared to take any schtick that might come from the other players on the mistakes you make and be able to cope with all the pressures that are put upon you," Connell said. "After that I would say you have to be a good defender. In that respect, I mean you have to tackle well, have the ability to read situations, and know how to position yourself to cover anything that gets past your fellow defenders, and recover quickly if a forward beats you. The more experience you have, the better."

From his youth experience playing forward, Connell knows that when a striker has the ball within 18-25 yards of the goal, he may offer you a tackling opportunity. "If the forward gets in that area with the ball, he loses a little bit of concentration because he's now thinking about having a shot on goal. That's the time you get your foot into a tackle or delaying process."

When a forward has the ball inside the 18-yard box, tackle him standing up. Avoid slide tackles, except in desperation situations, because your opponent may take a dive hoping the referee will be fooled and award him a penalty kick.

You can still tackle him hard standing up. "I wait until the player loses control, then I go in just when he's about to regain control of the ball again," Connell explained. "I tackle with the side of my foot with the force of my body following me. I put everything into it. That's the way I tackle hard."

Besides tackling well, a sweeper must also be able to dribble, pass, and shoot. Many teams now play with the sweeper overlapping forward when he has the opportunity to contribute in his forwards' attack on the opponents' goal.

"To overlap you have to be confident of your skills because every skill comes into play," Connell emphasized. "You have to be able to dribble past players. You want to make good passes, playing wall passes up the field. In between passes, you have to look around to see who's free so that when you get the ball back, it'll be a one touch pass to the next player. If you get an opportunity to shoot, you want to score."

When the team practices, he likes the sessions to be conducted in a happy atmosphere. "If you enjoy yourself, you will concentrate more and you'll be able to do things easier," Connell explained. "For me I'm always out to enjoy practice and have a good time. On the other hand, I always work hard at practice, like things I might be struggling on. I am always fully involved."

To get the most out of practices, Connell prefers small-group situations rather than drills.

"Five-aside games are very important in practices because not only does it give you a lot of confidence, but it also puts you in situations that do happen in games," he said. "Because you're playing on a smaller pitch, you think quicker, which gives you a couple of extra seconds in a regular game to do what you have thought about doing. I particularly like four-against-defense and stuff like that. Unless you are sorting things out, it's a waste of time."

Five-aside games can be used for skill and technique development. One variation of the game is to limit the players to two touches and later to one touch of the ball. In another game the player with the ball has to dribble past somebody before he can pass the ball or shoot.

"There are a lot of things you can do in five-aside that will help the team and help your aspects of the game," Connell said. "The most important thing about it is that you are enjoying yourself. As long as you are enjoying yourself, you are going to learn more and pick things up that much easier."

He also recommends players practice lots of shooting.

To be a good soccer player, you must have a good attitude. Connell believes a super attitude encompasses five qualities. "They are motivation, dedication, improvisation, imagination, and concentration. If you understand those five words and can relate to all five, then you have the right frame of mind and it's only the breaks you need from then on."

Bob Lenarduzzi
Vancouver Whitecaps

At age 25, fullback and midfielder Bob Lenarduzzi is already a respected nine-year veteran in professional soccer.

The Vancouver Whitecaps defender/midfielder can attribute much of his quick success to growing up in a soccer-playing family with his father and two brothers all active on the soccer pitch.

Born on May 1, 1955 in Vancouver, Lenarduzzi started playing soccer at age nine in the Grandview Legion, the juvenile soccer organization in Vancouver. He played in the league until age fifteen. He received a lot of coaching from his brother Sam.

"Ever since I was a kid I wanted to be a professional soccer player and the opportunity arose through the coach of Reading (England) being in Vancouver for the summer," Lenarduzzi said. "He was doing some coaching clinics. He saw me play and asked if I'd be interested in a tryout, and that's how it all came about."

Because he was only fifteen years old, his parents hesitated but finally agreed to let him go to England. Soon he was in reserve team, and even played in one first team game while still only fifteen years old. Still in the reserves the following season, he played about five first-team games. He became a full professional player at age seventeen and played with Reading from 1972 to 1977.

When the Whitecaps were formed in 1974, Lenarduzzi returned to Vancouver to play on loan from Reading. "It was just an ideal opportunity for me to come home. I never really settled there, I always wanted to come back here," Lenarduzzi said. "Playing for the Whitecaps was an ideal opportunity for me to play professional soccer and be happy as well, by playing in my own hometown."

In Vancouver's first season, Lenarduzzi started off playing center halfback and then right fullback. In 1978, he moved back up to midfield because the regular midfielder was injured. He played the midfield position very well and ended up playing the whole season there, scoring ten goals and seventeen assists.

"I started off in midfield again in 1979 and through necessity moved back to left fullback because we didn't have a player for that position," Lenarduzzi said. "I guess I'm a bit of a utility player really because I've played pretty well every position on the field except for goalkeeper."

In 1977 the Whitecaps purchased his contract from Reading. In 1978 he was chosen North American Player of the Year in the NASL, the first Canadian to achieve that honor. In 1979, Lenarduzzi was selected again for the North American All-Star Team and also for the NASL All-Star Second Team.

Lenarduzzi gained a lot of benefits playing in Reading's youth and reserve programs. "I think the biggest thing I learned was my knowledge of the game because we had soccer twenty-four hours a day," he explained. "I trained in the morning with the first team. Then in the afternoon, they'd have us back practicing different skills; trapping, heading, shooting. It was just soccer every day and I think that really helped my reading of the game, knowing what to do in certain situations and what not to do."

One tactic the Reading coaches ingrained in Lenarduzzi was knowing when and how to cover for a sweeper or centerhalf. "If their opposing goalie kicks the ball out of his hands and it goes up the middle, if one of our center halfbacks goes for the ball, I'd drop off at a forty-five degree angle to the centerhalf who's heading the ball, so it'd be like a triangle. There'd be my centerhalf heading the ball, there'd be me, and then there'd be my winger out wide. So if their player heads the ball out wide, I've got enough time to get out there," he said. "If their player heads it out over and behind our centerhalf, I've got enough time to get around and sweeper and cover, do whatever I have to do."

If the ball comes down near the halfway line, then you can drop back about twenty yards behind the centerhalf. If the ball is kicked deep into your half of the field, then ten yards is about the maximum distance you would drop behind your centerhalf.

Wall-pass situations can be sometimes difficult to defend against. If an opposing winger brings the ball down the line and one of his forwards or midfielders is running square or a little bit ahead of him, just stay with your man.

"Some inexperienced players will follow the ball and forget about their man and by that time the guy is behind them and gone," Lenarduzzi explained. "So what you do is as soon as the guy is coming toward you with the ball, watch him. If he passes the ball inside, forget about the ball, where it's gone, because you know a teammate is supporting you. Just run with your man, stay with him."

If you keep your opponent marked, the inside forward with the ball cannot pass it back to him. If he does, you can tackle the ball away before the winger gets it. Always try to channel your opponent outside.

While Lenarduzzi plays both defender and midfielder, his primary position is right fullback. Since the style of play of midfielders and defenders are not the same, he takes a different approach to playing each position.

"When I play midfield on offense, I play the type of position where I move out to wing and become pretty well a right winger," Lenarduzzi explained. "When we are defending, I drop back into midfield and just try to get behind the ball. Playing midfield involves a lot of running because I link up with the offense when we are attacking, and as soon as we lose the ball, I try to get back behind on the ball and link with the defense.

"When I play fullback, it's the same sort of thing, but less attacking because as the left fullback, your first concern is

Bob Lenarduzzi (5)

defending and anything you do going forward is a bonus. So
I try to attack as much as I can, but I don't do three-quarters
of the attacking I do in the midfield. If I'm playing left fullback and there's a winger there, my main concern is to stop
him, and as I say, anything going forward is a bonus."

To get his mind centered on the game, Lenarduzzi starts
concentrating about half an hour before the match. "I think
about the game and think positively that we're going to win.
I never think that we're going to lose," he said. "I concentrate on doing the right thing, the simple things. I'm not the

type of player where I'm going to get the ball and beat six people. I think to myself, 'Get the ball and play it simple and support other people.' I don't really need to get myself hyped up because I love playing so much that takes care of itself and I just enjoy being out there."

Every game starts with a clean balance sheet of 0-0. If you and the other defenders keep the other team scoreless during the first half, then you have done your job. If you stop the other team from scoring in the second half, you have done an outstanding job. "That's how I approach the game as a defender, by going out there and keeping the sheet clean," Lenarduzzi said.

You must know how to mark an opponent to prevent him from beating you with the ball. If the winger dribbles down from the thirty-five-yard line, and you are ten to twenty yards away, get close to him right away. If you do not put him under pressure, he will try to create a scoring opportunity. Get close enough to tackle if your opponent loses control of the ball, but not so close that if he pushes the ball past you, you cannot recover and mark him. While some defenders will stay about two yards off an opponent, Lenarduzzi closes in to about a yard of the winger.

"If you're confident enough that you can get a tackle in right away, get right on top of the player," he said. "So you know that if he's going to make a mistake, you're going to be able to pounce on it right away."

If you run at him head on, face to face, the winger can beat you on either side, to the right or to the left. If you channel him, approach him at about a 45-degree angle, he will probably move in the opposite direction. If you channel him from the right, he will dribble to the left. If he tries to come inside, then he will run straight into you. Dictate to him what you want him to do.

"If he's coming down the left wing (your right side), force him one way. Overemphasize one way so he has to go down the line," Lenarduzzi said. "You're running sideways, ready to tackle as soon as he pushes the ball to break into a sprint. Always lead with your right foot when playing right fullback. When you feel that you can tackle the ball away, flip your right foot around and make the tackle."

If you are about to channel an opponent outside to the right and one of your teammates behind you shouts to bring him inside to the left, move to your right, giving your opponent the space to come inside. Your teammate will be there waiting to tackle him. As soon as the winger speeds past you, turn and sprint around behind your teammate, in the off chance that the winger gets past him.

"You've always got to be aware of both your man and the ball," Lenarduzzi explained. "Say a man is coming down the middle of the field with the ball and your winger is standing wide. Concentrate on the ball first, that's where the most danger is at that time. Move into the middle and cover the centerback who is taking on the man with the ball. Be just off to the side behind him, at about a 45-degree angle."

Some players make the mistake of watching the ball and forgetting about their opponent. In that situation, the opponent in the middle can pass the ball out to the winger who can create a scoring opportunity before you can recover and stop him.

Although your team may play with four in the back, one of the fullbacks may have to cover the sweeper's position. If the opposing team plays two forwards right up the middle, the centerback and sweeper will have to mark them, leaving your team without a sweeper to roam around free in back. If an opposing forward breaks through down your right side, the left fullback will have to sweep.

"One of the center halves will be the covering man and I'll just push across and pick his man up. If the ball is coming down our right side, the least-dangerous man is the winger on my side then, because I have enough time to get from the middle of the field out to pressure my man if they knock the ball over to him," Lenarduzzi said. "All you do if the ball is coming down your right side is shuffle across one player. One of the centerhalves goes out and covers the fullback, and I'll come in and pick his man up."

If you have come inside, then your winger opponent runs inside, and none of your fellow defenders can mark him, you have to decide which player is more dangerous at that instant. If they are close together, try to mark them both by staying in between them.

"If a guy's coming down the middle with the ball, all four defenders want him to push the ball out wide," Lenarduzzi said. "We want to channel him outside, so we're building like we have a semi-circle starting with the left fullback sort of behind the two centerhalves. The right fullback will also be doing the same thing. He'll tuck in and it'll be like a semi-circle then. If the guy with the ball takes the two centerhalves on, the fullbacks should be there to cover or go out wide, if he hits the ball out to a winger. You want the ball out wide because that's where the ball is least dangerous."

If an opposing midfielder has the ball in the middle of the field and your winger streaks down the line, you still want to be covering inside. Since you are probably only about twenty yards away from the winger, if the midfielder passes the ball to him, you can sprint those twenty yards and take him on. If the opposing right midfielder has the ball and the right winger sprints down the line, stay within five or ten yards of the winger.

"The biggest thing in two-on-one is to try and delay them so it'll enable your teammates to get back. If you can hold them back that long, then you've done a good job," Lenarduzzi said. "By playing him wide, you should have bought yourself time to get your teammates back, but even if they aren't back yet, at least the guy with the ball is less dangerous out wide than he is in the middle in front of the goal."

If you can tackle the ball away, then tackle and clear it. Do not slide tackle unless you are 100 percent certain that you can get the ball. If you commit yourself in a slide tackle and miss, your opponent will be ten yards or more down the field with the ball before you can recover.

"When you slide tackle, you slide in on your backside, your left foot is hooked under your backside, and your right foot is forward to make the tackle," Lenarduzzi explained. "You don't leap into the air, just slide directly down on your backside. Swing your right leg into the tackle. Your right leg is rigid at the time of contact with the ball. If it isn't, if you're dangling it, you're not going to have that much power. Hook the instep of your right foot around the ball. If you have to struggle for it, then just strip your opponent of the ball by kicking it out wide."

Lenarduzzi trains the same way he plays in a game. "You can pick up a lot of bad habits in training by not doing it properly," he explained. "If you start doing things in training that you don't do in a game, such as passing the ball inside when you know you shouldn't, you may start doing it in a game. Always train to improve yourself. Make it enjoyable and have fun."

David D'Errico
San Diego Sockers

Renowned for his positive attitude and quest for learning, San Diego Socker defender David D'Errico is a natural leader and player. He has proven his versatility on the field during the last six NASL seasons having played midfielder, right fullback, centerback, left fullback, and sweeper. Born in Newark, New Jersey on June 3, 1952, he was named All-American at Hartwick College and captained the U.S. National Team in 1977.

The first ten to fifteen minutes of a game are very important for D'Errico in establishing his pattern of play.

"When I go out on the field, it initially becomes almost completely mental in terms of assessing my opponent's physical and technical abilities, his skill level, his strengths and weaknesses, what's he able to do," he explained. "If I'm going to play against a big, tall player, I have to be aware he may be very good in the air. I've got to see what kind of ball skills and speed he has. From there I have to adjust my own style of play."

At the same time he assesses his opponent, D'Errico makes sure the forward knows he is playing against a tough defender. Besides marking the forward tight and tackling hard, he will force the forward into playing a defensive role.

"I'm going to make him work as hard as I am. When I get the ball, he has to defend against me so he is not just standing up on the line all the time waiting for his team to give him the ball," he emphasized. "If he doesn't work defensively against me, then I'm going to be a free man and run up my side of the field with the ball, overlap, counterattack."

Because D' Errico is an imaginative player, defenders have difficulty predicting his next move. He feels his style brings out both the best of his ability and his opponent's ability. "I try to be as positive as possible, using as much imagination and improvisation as I can. He's going to have to bring his level up to mine or I'll beat him every time."

By forcing the forward to play the best he can, D'Errico believes this helps him play his best game. If the forward starts beating him, he views this as a challenge, motivating him to achieve an even higher level of play.

His positive attitude is with him every minute of the game. "I feel good about myself. I feel good about my strengths. I have a worth as a person first, and then I transfer that worth into my playing. I am able to do things, complete tasks, that make me feel good," he said.

The true test of positive attitude and self-confidence occurs when things go wrong. If that happens, D' Errico uses positive reinforcement. If you are depressed or not playing well during a game, do everything on a plus-minus basis. When you make a good pass or tackle, that is a plus. If you make a bad pass or miss heading the ball, that is a minus. The idea is to play so you earn yourself pluses on everything you do. The more pluses you achieve the better you feel about yourself and the way you play. Pretty soon you are totally involved in the game and playing at your best level.

"You can learn from the negatives, learn from something you did incorrectly," he advised. One way to do this is to use what he calls a 'self-evaluative training method' that works like this: if you kick a ball against the wall and it goes the wrong way off the side of your foot, ask yourself, "What part of my foot hit the ball? Was I watching the ball? Was my gravity over the ball? Where did my foot end up when I kicked the ball?" By recognizing your mistakes and correcting them, you will improve yourself.

"The difference between a mediocre player and a really

good player is that the mediocre player continues to repeat his mistakes, while the really good player corrects his mistakes and builds new strengths and positives," he said.

D' Errico has been a self-motivated player since he started playing soccer at age six in Harrison, New Jersey where he grew up. Because his mother supported the family of eight children and herself, they were quite poor.

"There was a lot of love in our family. It really helped keep us together," he said.

He played soccer for his grammar school as well as his youth league team. He also tried playing a little football and basketball, but neither sport appealed to him.

D'Errico and his friends enjoyed soccer so much they played it all year, even in the snow. "The cold and wetness didn't bother us because we were having so much fun," he recalled.

Since soccer was already a popular sport in New Jersey, a lot of talented players tried out for the Harrison High School soccer teams. Rising above the stiff competition, D' Errico earned himself a position on the junior varsity team in his freshman year and made the varsity team in his sophomore year.

After high school he attended Mercer Junior College in New London, Connecticut for two years where he was named All-American. Transferring to Hartwick College in his junior year, he made All-American in his senior year. Chosen to play in the 1973 Senior Bowl for the East Squad, he was named Most Valuable Defensive Player of the game. After his graduation in 1974, he was the first round draft pick and third overall in that year's college draft by the Seattle Sounders. After a stint in the reserves, he played in the first team through the 1976 season. Then he was traded to the Minnesota Kicks.

When he broke his leg in two places during the 1977 preseason, the doctors told him he might never play professional soccer again. D' Errico devised his own recovery program taken from doctor's advice and research material he had studied on his own. With his left leg still in a cast, he was soon exercising daily; riding a stationary bike, lifting weights, swimming, and riding a bicycle thirty miles on weekends.

David D'Errico (2)

His penchant for learning served him well in developing his recovery program because he had studied muscle development. His desire to play again was his chief motivation.

"My first objective was to walk without a limp," he recalled. "The second was to jog without a limp, and then sprint without a limp. When I achieved that, my goals were to run from side to side, check, and finally do everything without a limp."

Within nine weeks he was back on the soccer field and two weeks later he played in a regular game. During the offseason, he captained the U.S. National Team which won the Tournament of the Americans. In 1978 he played for the New England Tea Men and then indoor soccer with the Cincinnati Kids before signing with the Rochester Lancers in 1979. He joined the San Diego Sockers in 1980.

Since every player needs to see and be aware of everyone and everything happening around him on the field, D' Errico recommends that you try to improve your peripheral vision.

"When you walk down the street, take a quick glance right or left as fast as you can, look forward again, and mentally tell yourself what you have just seen. Maybe you saw a tree, a bush, a person wearing a red shirt walking down the street. Now take a look at where you glanced and see what is actually there," he suggested. "Keep developing your peripheral vision this way, looking right, left, behind you, and forward. I think this helps you immensely to improve your ability to see players around you and know what is going on."

D' Errico believes every fullback should have positional sense. "Say a winger is dribbling down the left wing against the right fullback. The right fullback has to learn to cover behind the centerback," he explained. "If the winger floats the ball over the back post, over the centerback, the left fullback has to get the ball out of the danger area."

If the ball is crossed from the left wing into the middle of the field, the left fullback has to close down the play and hold the right winger outside away from the ball.

Fullbacks should always be on their toes, never on their heels. "If he is on his heels, he's off balance. All the striker has to do is put one move on him and the guy is left behind," he explained. "If you are on your heels, you have no quickness on the turn because you're unbalanced. You'll get beaten every time."

To tackle well, you must have patience. You must quickly assess whether you can get the ball or should just force him to play the ball back to a midfielder. If the forward with the ball has his back to your goal and you just go in for a hasty tackle, the forward can also make a quick move with the ball to the other side and dribble past you. "Only tackle when you are positive you can take the ball away," he advised.

"You must try new things in practices because that's when you have the most freedom for improvisation. If you don't try things out in practice you'll never try them in a game."

When an opponent brings the ball into your half of the field, you should try to channel him wide to the outside. If you can prevent the forward from dribbling the ball or passing it into the center of the field in front of the goal, you have eliminated a lot of problems for your fellow defenders and your goalkeeper.

"If the forward has the ball, I have to determine when I can go in and win the ball. If I don't feel I can win the ball, then I'll hold him, meaning that I'll position my body to prevent him from coming inside," he explained. "I'll approach him on my toes, from about 5-6 yards, being ready to tackle when I have the opportunity. Approach him at a 60-80 degree angle, depending on his speed and skill. The faster and more skilled he is, the bigger the angle you give him, like 80 degrees."

Make him play down the touchline. The closer he is to the touchline, the less operating room he has to try to maneuver around you. Always concentrate on the ball. Avoid watching his body movements because they will distract you from his next move.

"Obviously, his function is to put me off balance. One way is to make an intentional move, go one way and then go the other. So if I'm watching his body instead of the ball, it'd be easy for him to put me off balance and get by me with the ball. So I have to concentrate on the ball at all times," he said. "I also have to use my peripheral vision to see what is happening around me which will help me assess his next move."

If you run square towards him at a 90 degree angle, you give him too many options. He can dribble down the touchline, come inside, pass the ball inside, take you on one-on-one, or pass it back to the midfielder. When you approach him diagonally at a 60-80 degree angle, you reduce the number of options he has. He cannot dribble inside unless he wants to play you one-on-one. He will have difficulty passing the ball inside because you are in the way. Besides taking you on, he can only dribble down the touchline or pass back to his midfielder.

If you approached the forward straight on, face to face, he could try to move on either side of you. He would enjoy almost the same options he would have if you came at him from a 90 degree angle. If you approach him diagonally from a 60-80 angle from the right, his best option is to go left. If you want him to go right, approach him diagonally from the left.

"When you're channeling the player, you're trying to slow him down, hold him up, lessen his opportunities," he emphasized. "If the player is coming with the ball down the wing and you faced him straight on, he'd have a lot of passing range. When you've narrowed his options down to either dribbling down the sideline or passing back, you can concentrate on tackling and winning the ball."

To tackle, watch the ball, keep your arms out for balance, knees bent to keep your center of gravity low for power. Set your distance by how good the forward is. If he is fast and skillful, keep a larger distance than normal. Tackle with 100 percent conviction and tackle through the ball.

A positive mental committment is important in tackling the ball away from an opponent. "If you're afraid that you might get hurt in tackling, then you're going to get hurt," he said. "You have to say to yourself, 'I'm going in and win the ball,' and then do it."

Before going into the tackle, you should know where your teammates are. If one of your midfielders is open in front of you, when you tackle the ball, pass it directly to him. Your awareness and quickness gives your team the advantage in launching a counterattack.

In practice sessions, try different things like tackling and passing at the same time. "Concentrate and dedicate yourself to achieving the goals you set," D' Errico explained. "Learn something new every day. When you're coming up level to level, improving yourself, retain that good feeling about yourself, that confidence, 'Hey, you're a good person.' That will help you in everything you do in life."

Before you start a practice, determine a goal you want to achieve that session. "I try and learn something new or improve on something each day. This helps me become a better player and a better person. It may be tackling, curling the ball, communication with other players, or anything else.

I have a responsibility to myself to improve my weaknesses and build my strengths."

D' Errico believes every soccer player should be committed to a goal of becoming the best player he possibly can. If certain sacrifices have to be made to provide time for soccer practice and games, like eliminating dilly dallying after school, then sacrifices have to be made. When he practices and plays he must concentrate his energies on learning new things, developing his skills, using his imagination and creativity.

"He must dedicate himself, have a dream," he said. "My perception is a player who, instead of messing around after school, goes home and does his homework and his chores. He does them correctly the first time to avoid wasting time and energy. Then he's out doing his soccer, and doing it well, picking up very good habits, feeling good about himself, doing the correct job at the right time, picking up new ideas, and always trying to do his best."

Part Four

The Goalkeepers

Bill Irwin
Washington Diplomats

With a 1.45 goals against average for the 1979 NASL season, Washington Diplomats goalkeeper Bill Irwin has proven that his style of emphasizing basics reaps large rewards.

Unlike many professional netminders who played other positions before entering the goal, Irwin has played goalkeeper since he started playing soccer at school in Donaghadee, a village near where he was born in Northern Ireland on July 23, 1951. "I've always been happy in goal," he said, "I always look forward to playing there."

Besides playing on his school team, Irwin also played for the Boys Brigade (which is similar to our Boy Scouts). Since two soccer fields were within a few minutes walk from his home, Irwin and his friends spent their afternoons playing soccer.

At age 16, he started playing semiprofessional soccer. Since Northern Ireland had no professional league, the semiprofessional players both worked and played. When he played for Bangor, coach Ralph McQuicken discussed his performance after each game, telling him how to improve for the next match. When Charlie Tully became the Bangor coach, he helped Irwin get a try-out in England. Later, he was bought by Cardiff City in Wales, signed a professional contract, and played with the club from 1972 until early 1978 when the Washington Diplomats purchased his contract.

Cardiff coach Jimmy Scouler helped give him the will to win. "Before I knew Jimmy Scouler, it didn't make any difference whether we won in a practice game because it was just practice," Irwin recalled. "But he'd want to win every game. He set an example for me that gave me this will to always want to win my games. I have a lot of respect for the man."

After his first season with the Dips in 1978, Irwin set a new club record for lowest goals-against average of 1.49, most saves with 178, most minutes played with 2,362 minutes, and most games played (27). He also received All-NASL Honorable Mention honors. During the 1979 season, he brought his goals-against average down to 1.45 for another club record.

One technique Irwin learned in his youth career which he still uses today to narrow his angle is the arc. The arc is a half of a circle with a goalpost at either end of the half circle.

To learn how the arc is used, pound a stake in the middle of the goal line and tie a 9-yard rope to it. The length of the rope actually depends on the distance you normally come out from goal, usually somewhere between six yards and the penalty spot 12 yards away. Hold the end of the rope and walk straight out in front of the goal until it stops you. This is the tip of your arc, the greatest distance forward your rope will reach from the goal.

Now move to your right. Notice that as you move to the right, the length of rope pulls you back a bit. Continue moving to the right until you reach the right post. Be sure that you are not beyond the right post nor much inside it. Now swing back to the center of the arc, straight out in front of center of the goal line. With the rope still tied to the stake, swing around to the left until you reach the left goalpost. Again, you should not find yourself outside the left goalpost nor should you be much inside the left goalpost.

"If the forward moves over to the left, just go a bit across like you're on an arc," Irwin explained. "When your near post is covered he can't beat you. The better your angle, the better chance you have of making the save."

To gain an even better understanding of angles, have a forward with the ball stand about eighteen to twenty yards out from the goal line. Draw an imaginary line from the stake in the middle of your goal line to the forward. Keep the rope end in your hand and move out to the edge of your arc, and position yourself along the imaginary line between the forward and the center of the goal line. This will help you determine just where on the arc you should be each time the forward moves right or left.

When the forward with the ball attacks the goal from eighteen to twenty yards out, move out and narrow the angle, all the time remembering your arc if he moves right or left. Use the imaginary line to guide you, and always cover your near post.

If you reach the edge of your arc, do not stop if there is still more room to narrow your angle and close him down. "You just can't say I'm going out nine yards and that's it. It all depends on the individual situation, like the control the fellow has on the ball, and whether you think you can get it," he said.

In a game situation where an opposing winger brings the ball down the touchline and his center forward runs down the middle toward your goal, watch the opponent with the ball. If the winger cuts inside with the ball toward the goal and there are no defenders marking either the winger or the center forward, you have to concentrate on the winger because he has the ball.

"Even though it's a two-on-one situation, I can't go between them because that'd give the winger an opportunity to score. You've got to treat it like a one-on-one situation," he said. "Narrow your angles and play your arc just as though the center forward wasn't there. You've got to take the man with the ball because the ball is the danger. You sort of shut the center forward out of your mind and concentrate on that ball."

If the winger passes the ball to the center forward, there

is not much you can do about it, except dive after the ball or swing around on your arc and try to cut down the center forward's angle before he can shoot.

"If the winger gets the ball down to the midfield line and starts to dribble in along the byline toward the goal, position yourself tight against your near post," Irwin said. "If he takes a shot on goal, you're going to make a save. If he chips it to the far post, all you do is turn and get across to the far side as quick as possible."

When the opposing team has the ball about thirty-five yards from goal and your fullbacks are around the top of your 18-yard box, you should probably be two to three yards off your line. Be sure that you position yourself between the forward with the ball and your goal, in case he tries to drive a power shot or you want to rush out and narrow your angle, if he breaks through your fullbacks.

If the forward with the ball gets down to your 25-yard line, you should still be two to three yards off your line. Do not come out further because your fullbacks are closing him down and trying to tackle and get the ball away.

Playing angles is an essential part of goalkeeping and you must always keep your eye on the ball. A goalkeeper figures his angle by imagining a forward with a ball running towards the goal. Say he is about twelve yards from the center of the goal line. Draw an imaginary line from the right goalpost to the attacker, and the goal line between the two goalposts. The three lines form a triangle with the forward at the top.

The triangle shows you the total shooting area the forward has on the goal. If you stand in the center of the goal line, you see how much space on either side of you the forward has to shoot through. If he kicks the ball too close to you, you can easily save it. The nearer he hits the ball to the goalposts, the harder it is for you to save it. If you step out four yards toward the forward, he has less space on either side of you to kick the ball into the back of the goal because you have narrowed the angle. The closer you get to him, the less angle he has to shoot.

"If you can keep your angles right, it cuts down the size of the target for the forward," he said. "I was always taught

Bill Irwin

never be beaten on your near post, the goalpost nearest the ball. It should be covered all the time."

If the forward is in front of the right goalpost, that is your near post. If he moves across to the left side, the left goalpost becomes your near post.

"If you stand on your line you've got no real angle at all because that presents the striker with a full size of the goal to hit. But if you move off your line, say a yard, it cuts down the size of the target, and it makes it harder for him to score," Irwin explained. "All he sees is maybe you and doesn't see very much of the target."

Always try to make yourself as big a target as possible because this makes the goal look small to the striker. Keep on your toes, ready to spring, and spread your hands out away from your body, but not enough to impair your balance. Crouch, bend over a little bit, but just enough that you do not lose your image of being big.

When the ball is in the opposing team's half of the field, Irwin will position himself between the six-yard line and the penalty spot. The distance the goalkeeper comes off his line depends on his height; a short goalkeeper will probably not come out as far as Irwin, who is six-feet, three-inches tall.

When the ball is in play at the other end of the field, watch it and adjust your position to it. "If the play is at the other end, you're not out of the game. That is a crucial time for a goalkeeper concentration-wise," he emphasized. "If you let your concentration wander, and not think about the ball, that's when you're going to get caught out. I think when the play is at the other end, you should be more mentally on your toes than if the play is all at your end."

If you fail to watch the ball and let your mind drift away, like watching the crowd or wondering if it could rain, you may be caught out of position if the ball is suddenly played into your half of the field. If your concentration is broken, the other team may score before you can center yourself and get into position to make the save.

If the other team brings the ball down close enough for a long 30-40 yard chip shot, you need to take four to five steps back just to get into position to prevent the ball passing over your head into the back of the net. You must concentrate and be prepared for anything that might happen.

"One of the best bits of advice I got as a youth player was always watch the ball," he recalled. "The ball is going to come to you, you won't have to go to it. That's a piece of advice that has stood me good since I first heard it."

Arnie Mausser
Ft. Lauderdale Strikers

Arnie Mausser's quickness and six foot two inch height have made him almost unbeatable in the air against crosses and corner kicks. Before being acquired by the Ft. Lauderdale Strikers prior to the 1979 season, Mausser had played on a different team each season since he began his professional soccer career in 1974.

Born and raised in Brooklyn, New York, Mausser started learning soccer at about age seven. By age ten, he was playing soccer all year around, trying various positions including winger, fullback and centerback. He didn't start goalkeeping until he was in the eighth grade.

"Our substitute goalkeeper didn't show up for a game so we had no backup. So they put me in goal," he recalled. "I had a good match so I've been in there ever since."

During high school, Mausser's coach occasionally would let him play forward when his team had a comfortable lead. This experience proved valuable to his goalkeeping game as well. "It (playing in the field) gives me more confidence when I have to kick the ball out, pass the ball or come out of the penalty area to clear it," he explained. "I think playing elsewhere helps you to read the game better. You know what's going on in the shooter's mind and what to look for when he takes a shot."

Mausser spent most of his youth experience in the Cosmopolitan League in which many teams stayed together for years, and thus developed good communication and teamwork. Mausser played in the league throughout high school and college because it offered him better competition than the school leagues. He earned his B.A. degree in Business Administration at Queens College in 1974. Upon graduation, he joined the American Soccer League Rhode Island Oceaneers and moved to the North American Soccer League in 1975. His former NASL clubs include Connecticut Bicentennials, Tampa Bay Rowdies, Vancouver Whitecaps, and Colorado Carribou.

Although he has moved from club to club, Mausser's experience, consistency and all around ability has gained him a reputation for reliability around the league. He also has put in a number of international performances as goalkeeper for the U.S. National Team. In 1976 he was selected the Most Valuable North American Player in the NASL.

Mausser credits his good record to knowing how to read the game and practicing fundamental goalkeeping techniques. There are some basics that every keeper should learn and practice as he works his way up through the ranks.

During the first few minutes of a game, Mausser watches the opposing forwards to see whether they shoot right- or left-footed or both, whether they like to bend balls, or whatever characteristics he can pick up in playing against them.

"Try to get into the game as much as possible right away. Concentrate on the game," Mausser advised. "You can't take your mind off the game. Don't bother with the people on the sidelines, don't let them distract you."

Besides concentration, a goalkeeper also needs courage and bravery, especially in one-on-one situations with an opposing forward. While you might get a few bruises taking the ball off an opponent's foot, "it hurts worse when the ball goes into the net," Mausser said. "If you stop it, then nobody worries about it. It's like making a great save when you hurdle yourself across the goal. It feels good when you prevent the guy from scoring."

To stop a power shot from twenty or more yards away, keep your eye on the ball, especially when the forward kicks it. "You watch the ball all the way. This way you can move over to the left or right and get your body between the ball and the goal. Get your hands behind it like you would any other shot.

If the ball is hit hard chest high, try to catch it with your chest absorbing the impact of the shot. If a power shot is hit high, knock it away from you toward the sidelines instead of trying to catch and hold onto it. If the forward kicks a low, hard shot, just cutting the top of the grass, bend your knees and collapse on the ball, Mausser said.

"Throw your body down, like diving right across the goal," he explained. "Get as much of your body behind the ball as you can. Collapse on your side, try to get your chest behind the ball, and have your hands ready to pull it into your chest."

When a forward tries to curl a ball, bend it with a banana kick, you watch the ball very closely. "You have to pick up the direction of the ball the second it leaves the player's foot. That's why it is very important to keep your eye on the ball," Mausser said. "A bend isn't a hard shot most of the time, it's sort of a tap, like a little floater. You'll see if it bends, and you'll be able to anticipate what direction the ball is going. It's just a matter of anticipation and watching the ball."

You must also know where you are in relation to your goalposts as well as knowing where the ball is. Then you will know whether the ball has a chance of going into the goal. You must react instantly and get into positon to make the save.

According to Mausser, you can look at the shooter's feet to tell what direction he wants to hit the ball. See what direction his planted foot, his standing foot, is pointed in because that is the direction he will kick the ball.

"Try it yourself. If you want to shoot the ball to the left, you point the foot you stand on to the left," he said. "Your standing foot is supposed to be next to the ball, right? Try pointing your standing foot to the right and kick the ball to the left. You can't get anything behind the ball. It's a pretty awkward position. You look at a player's backswing too, how he brings his foot back, and then strikes the ball.

If he hits the ball with the outside of his right instep, he might try and bend the ball to his right. If he strikes the ball with the inside of his instep, he wants to curl the ball to his left. The opposite directions will be true, if he hits the ball with his left foot.

If the shooter leans back when he kicks the ball with his instep, outside or inside the foot, he wants to chip the ball. If he leans forward with his body over the ball, the shot will be low.

When you come off the goal line to challenge the shooter, move out quickly, but cautiously. "You can't come out running crazy from the goal because you'd be off-balance. The shooter can just dribble around you. If he shoots while you're running, you have very little chance of stopping the ball because your momentum is going to carry you forward and you're not going to be able to react to the ball quick enough to dive effectively," Mausser explained. "Just before he kicks the ball, slow down, face him off, and crouch down a little bit in a basic stance. Be on your toes, balanced, really ready to dive to the left or right."

Sometimes the shooter will dribble the ball a few inches or even a foot too far in front. His loss of control gives you the opportunity to pounce on the ball, if you are close enough. Do not dive, if you are more than five feet away from the ball. If you dive too early, too far away from the ball, the forward will shoot the ball underneath you or dribble around you.

"The closer you get, the more chance you have of stopping it," Mausser said. "The best thing to do is spread yourself, go down on your side actually, and just slide into the ball. Watch the ball and get your body down fast in front of it. Come down parallel so that your shoulder and hip land on the ground at the same time. You want to come down diagonally forward to grab the ball."

Arnie Mausser

You want to come down fast to prevent the forward from shooting the ball beneath you during your dive. If he shoots, you want the ball to bounce off your chest, and hopefully, deflect far enough away that you can recover before another shot is taken.

If you dive and knock the forward off his feet, that is a legal tackle for a goalkeeper, even if you do not get the ball.

"Stretch yourself, spread and extend yourself as much as you can. Try to get as much of your body as possible in front of the ball so the shooter can't get around you," Mausser said. "Try to dive so you have the ball at the middle of your body. If he tries to dribble around you, you still have your hands to get the ball away or your legs and feet to knock it away.

"Hopefully, you have enough momentum to get the ball

before he has enough time to change his direction. He may make a mistake or panic which is to your advantage."

Try to fake the shooter into going the direction you want him to go. If he is coming down on your right, lean to the right and then reverse direction. The more he thinks about what you are doing, the less he can concentrate on what he wants to do.

When you reach for the ball, keep your wrists solid. If he shoots against your hands, get as much of your hands in front of the ball as you can. There will be enough resistance in your hands and wrists to knock the ball away. If he tries to chip the ball over you, slap it away.

If you can get your hands on the ball and hold onto it, clutch it tight against you, and roll up into a ball. Then the shooter cannot kick the ball out of your grasp.

"The main thing in diving is not to go down too quickly. Don't dive unless you're within four or five feet of the ball," Mausser said. "Come out fast when you come off the line. Slow down when you approach the ball. Keep slowing down until you dive. At the same time crouch over. The closer I get, the lower I get to the ground. If you want to be successful in diving, you have to practice. If you don't practice, you won't be effective at it."

When a winger dribbles the ball down the sideline and starts to cross the ball to his forwards in front of the goalmouth, Mausser positions himself about halfway between the goalposts.

"You don't want to be too close to the near post because if you do, the ball is going to be over your head," Mausser explained. "Judge how far the cross is coming, how high it is coming, and if you can get to it safely. So it's a matter of practicing taking crosses in the air constantly. Have teammates cross the ball, and practice catching balls at different angles with forwards pressuring you."

Be sure to watch the ball at all times. Once you have determined where and how the ball will pass over or by you, you have to jump and catch the ball at your highest point. If you wait for the ball to come down and catch it in your arms, a forward can get in front of you and head the ball into the goal.

"You've got to meet the ball," Mausser said. "You jump with your arms stretched above you. It's better to cut the ball off (catch) as soon as possible."

When you go to catch the ball, form the letter "W" with your hands. Spread your fingers apart with your thumbs almost touching. This gives you the widest surface to catch the ball. It also allows your hands to cushion the force of the shot. Try to catch the ball right in the middle of your hands. Gather it in and hold onto it.

"Usually when you pick up a cross, there's somebody free in the midfield because all their forwards are rushing onto the goalmouth when you cut the ball off," Mausser said. "As soon as you get the ball under control, throw it out to a midfielder who is open. It seems like you can always get a quick counterattack off a cross."

If you hesitate in launching the counterattack, the opposing players will rush back into their normal positions and your momentary advantage will be lost.

When your midfielders see you catch the cross, they should immediately run into open space in anticipation of your throw. This comes about through teamwork in practice and games.

If you are off-balance when the cross comes over or cannot jump up in time to catch it, punch the ball up and over the crossbar. The opposing team will gain a corner kick, but you have prevented the ball from going into the net.

"If the ball is wet or you don't think you can hang onto it, the best thing is to punch it as hard as you can, get some height and distance on it. Basically, punch the ball to the sidelines, do not knock it right up the middle where they can get it and attack right away again," he advised. "If the cross is hit low and you can't catch it because one of their forwards is in front of you shielding the ball with his body, punch it out. Sometimes it's the only thing you can do. You can't catch everything."

When you punch the ball, try to hit it with both fists.

Clench your fists and strike the ball like you would hit a punching bag. If you cannot get both fists on the ball, then put all your power into the one-fisted punch.

"The main thing is to watch the ball. You can't pay attention to where the forward is," Mausser explained. "Clear everything out of your mind and concentrate on the ball."

When the ball is in the opposing team's half of the field, Mausser will come out as far as the penalty area. Because of his height (he is six feet two) he is less concerned than most goalkeepers about a forward chipping a ball over his head.

"You're always careful about chips," he explained. "You can always tell when a forward is going to shoot or chip by the way he positions himself." If the forward has his body over the ball when he kicks it, the shot will be on the ground. If he leans back, then he will chip the ball in the air.

When an opposing player dribbles or passes the ball over the halfway line, Mausser positions himself behind the penalty spot, seven to eight yards from the goal line. If the forward dribbles a little to the left, you move to the left. If he moves right, you move right.

When an opposing winger gets the ball all the way down the touchline near the corner flag, he will probably try to cross the ball to his forwards in front of the goalmouth. Position yourself about halfway between the goalposts. You want to be flexible in either running forward or backing up to the far post. If the winger tries to bend the ball around the near post into the goal, sprint forward and save it. If you see the ball will go over your head, get back and protect the far post.

To help new keepers understand the concept of narrowing angles, take a long rope and tie each end to a goalpost.

"Have a guy pull the rope tight out to the penalty spot. Then have your goalkeeper walk slowly from the middle of the goal line out to the penalty spot," Mausser explained. "Every couple of steps have the goalkeeper look at the shooter on the penalty spot and then at each side of the rope, so he can see how much room there is between his body and each rope. The closer he gets to the shooter, the less space the guy has to shoot the ball into the goal. When the goalkeeper stands right in front of the shooter, he'll see that he's cut the angle to zero."

Then have the goalkeeper return to the goal line, stand a yard away from the right goalpost, and start walking toward the shooter standing on the penalty spot. Have the goalkeeper notice how much space there is between him and the left rope and how easy it would be for the shooter to score. The closer the goalkeeper moves to the middle and the shooter, the more he cuts the shooter's angle.

Next have the goalkeeper walk to the middle of the goal line and have the shooter move to the right, keeping the rope taut at his feet so that he is still the far point of the triangle. "Now have the goalkeeper move forward and to the right until he cuts the shooter's angle down. Remember that he should always protect his near post," he said. "Then do it without the rope. Keep working at it until you build a little bit of confidence."

The more confidence you have, the better you will play. "I think the biggest boost to any confidence is having good training sessions," Mausser said. "If you train well and conscientiously, it goes a long way to improving your confidence."

Mausser has a sharpness routine which every goalkeeper can use. First, kick the ball back and forth with a partner to loosen up. Then sit down in the middle of the goal and have your partner go out six to seven yards and shoot balls to the right and left of you, but close enough for you to reach out and catch them. Next have him push the ball close to a goalpost. You have to get up, go get it, throw it back to him, and sit back down in the middle of the goal before your partner pushes the ball to the opposite goalpost.

"It's pretty hard work, but it's the best thing. It increases your quickness," Mausser said. "You also want to work on your technique. Experiment with new things in practice. Then in games, concentrate, watch the ball closely, and anticipate what the shooter will do. Always work hard."

Alan Mayer
California Surf

Recognized as one of the most aggressive goalkeepers in the NASL, Alan Mayer is a natural athlete with outstanding reflexes and quickness. Born on July 3, 1952 in Islip, Long Island, New York, he played varisty soccer, tennis, and basketball in high school and college. After graduating from college in 1974, he was the number one draft choice of the Baltimore Comets. Mayer moved with the franchise to San Diego in 1976 when the team became the Jaws, and then to Las Vegas in 1977 where the club was renamed the Quick Silvers. He returned with the club to San Diego in 1978 where he played until 1980 when he moved to the California Surf. Among his numerous honors, Mayer was voted North American Player of the year by NASL players in 1978. Because of several concussions he has suffered since childhood, he wears a protective goal cap made of flexible rubber. He has played goalkeeper four years on the U.S. National Team.

Alan Mayer's aggressive style of goalkeeping has rewarded him with saving many shots that other goalkeepers would have failed to stop.

"When I'm in the goal I'm not afraid of any situation," he explained. "There's some goalkeepers that like to lay back and let the play develop for them, but a lot of times I like to go and develop the play myself. Whenever there is a 50-50 ball, I'll go in and do my darndest to get the ball. This means a lot of times you have to go in head first or go in feet first or throw your body in the way of the ball. In past seasons I would just go crazy and go get the ball. Now I rely on my experience to help me pick the right time to go and get the ball."

If two or three players rush in to kick the ball, Mayer will dive forward without his hands outstretched and make the save. "I guess courage has a lot to do with it," he noted. "If diving to make a save means taking a kick in the legs or body, then I would go ahead and do it. I think my biggest thing is the fact that I'm not afraid of any situation that's involved in a soccer game."

When you dive, go after the ball with your hands. "If you have the idea that you're going to come up with the ball, then you're going to succeed a lot of the time," he explained. "If there are too many legs and feet involved to give you much of a chance of making the save, then it's sometimes better if you go in with your feet to knock the ball out, just as you would as a field player making a tackle."

Preparation for a game is most important. If the game is scheduled for a Saturday, Mayer begins his physical preparation on Monday. "I like to do all my physical conditioning during the early part of the week and then work on my individual goalkeeping through the rest of the week," he said.

On Monday he conditions his body with calisthenics, sit-ups, and running. "The first few steps in a game are the most important ones," he said. "It's not how long you can last, it's your quick movement. So I feel a goalkeeper should work hard on his sprinting."

Instead of sprinting 100 yards, sprint 60-70 steps. You may find you can run eight or nine yards in four steps. Unless you practice your quick starts and sprints, you will not have that necessary burst of speed when you need it most in a game.

Goalkeepers should also do a lot of leg work. Mayer does a series of jumping back and forth over a ball to strengthen his legs. You should also work on jumping up and touching your knees to your chest. Not only does this help you jump higher for crosses, it also benefits your diving.

"The stronger your legs are, the further you're going to jump or dive," he said. "Half an inch sometimes means whether the ball goes into the net which could mean the game."

As the week progresses, concentrate on having a lot of shots taken at you. Have a partner throw a ball on one side of you and then the other. Dive after each ball, get back into position, and then dive on the next ball. Later put a ball in the middle of the goal and practice diving from side to side over it.

Slack off hard physical conditioning toward the end of the week. Practice taking crosses and playing in game situations. Work with your coach in scheduling a routine for the week which includes all the areas you want to improve and strengthen.

Mental preparation is even more important than physical preparation. "It's very important that you are mentally ready to play a game, that you're just not going in there and relying on your physical capabilities," he explained. "Goalkeeping is more mental than physical. You have to be alert all the time to do the things you are physically capable of doing. My mental game starts in the preseason and I don't get out of the mental state until the end of the season."

If a game is scheduled for Saturday, begin thinking about the game on Monday. As you taper off physical conditioning in the middle of the week, increase your mental concentration to a peak just before the game.

"As it comes towards game time, I'm constantly thinking about the game and what I will be doing in different situations, whether the ball comes high or it's a short kick or a one-on-one situation," he said. "I'm always trying to put different plays in my mind so that when the actual thing occurs in the game, not only am I physically ready, but I'm mentally alert for the play."

Mental preparation includes playing the game in your mind. When you are relaxed, picture different game situations, like a winger crossing the ball into the goalmouth area. See yourself go up and catch the ball. Then you might picture a one-

Alan Mayer

on-one situation with a forward doing a lot of feints, trying to get around you with the ball. See yourself dive and take the ball off his feet. Always be successful in every situation you picture.

Use your imagination to help you concentrate during games. "You have to play mental games with yourself to keep alert so when the ball does come down to you, you're able to react to the ball the way you want to," he advised.

When an opponent brings the ball into your third of the field, you must read the game and anticipate what could happen if your defender marking the opponent with the ball is beaten.

"You ask yourself questions like, 'If the forward with the ball goes on the outside of the defender, am I going to be able to get the ball? If he cuts inside, what do I do in that situation?' " he explained.

Since the goalkeeper is positioned behind the defenders, you can better see what's happening on the field around them. Keep a constant stream of communication flowing to them. If a forward has moved behind a fullback, tell your teammate where the opponent is. If you see a play developing that will catch your defenders unawares, advise them where to better position themselves.

"I talk constantly with my fullbacks to make them aware of situations that they might not be fully aware of," he said. "It's very important that the goalkeeper communicates with his defense."

Mayer did not start playing goalkeeper until he was 15, which was only the second season he had played the game. In grammar school he played all the other sports.

Because he did not have a preference for one sport over another, he played on organized teams in every major sport, except football. Soccer had not yet become popular in the area.

Mayer often dreamed of becoming a professional athlete. Unconcerned which sport he played, he always wanted to be a professional player. He held that dream all the way through high school and college.

In high school some of his friends invited him to come and play soccer. "I needed something to do in the fall because I played basketball and tennis," he explained. "I had to make a decision to play soccer or football. All my friends at the time were playing soccer so I just went out and started playing. I started on the forward line and played there for one year. The next season when our goalie let five goals in during a crucial game, the coach just came up to me and asked if I fancied playing.

"I said, 'Yeah, I'd love to give it a try' because all through growing up, I used to love diving after things. I thought that was neat. That was my sophomore year in high school. I've been in goal ever since."

During the summertime, his family spent a lot of time at the beach. He and his brother Bill played lots of frisbee, football, and volleyball on the sand. "I guess I really enjoyed the thrill of throwing myself around and making a catch where you've got to dive to make the catch when the football or frisbee is thrown a few feet away from you," he explained. "You can't catch it so you dive into the water and catch it or you dived along the beach. It was no fun when you dove and missed. It was a lot of fun when you dove and were able to catch whatever you were going after."

All the diving on the beach enhanced his natural athletic ability because his diving instincts were already formed when he first went into the goal.

After graduating from high school, he entered Madison College in Virginia where he played four years of varsity soccer and tennis. Mayer was selected the Most Valuable Player each year four years straight in both sports. He was twice made All American in soccer. Academically Mayer was a superior student all four years.

After graduation Mayer was the number one draft choice of the Baltimore Comets in 1974. He remained in goal for the franchise through all its moves from Baltimore to San Diego in 1976, Las Vegas in 1977, and back to San Diego in 1978. During the off-seasons in 1974 and 1975, he trained with Southend United in England. In a reserve team match, he earned the unique honor of scoring a goal when he kicked a long punt which skidded on the wet grass past the opposing goalkeeper into the back of the net.

Because he is a most aggressive goalkeeper and has suffered nine concussions since childhood, he started wearing a goalie cap. "After I received a concussion up in Portland early in the 1978 season, I started looking around in sporting goods stores to find a cap that would protect me," he said. "I found what I was looking for in a San Diego store, and with a few modifications, I've worn a goalie cap ever since then."

Made of soft foam rubber about an inch thick, the goalie cap resembles an old time football helmet and covers most of the head except for the face. Perforated with holes for ventilation, the goalie cap is so lightweight he forgets that he has it on.

He compares the goalie cap to the face mask worn by ice hockey goalies. People ridiculed the first ice hockey goalie who wore a mask, but after the players and fans realized the mask's value, every goalie wore one. Mayer hopes the same thing will happen in soccer.

One way a goalkeeper can protect himself against a charging forward when he jumps up to catch a ball in the air is to raise one knee when he jumps up. Any forward running into a goalkeeper's knee will avoid crashing into him again.

When the opposing team is awarded a free kick on your 35-yard line or closer, you should line up your players in a wall right away before an opponent can take the kick. To prevent the opponent from taking a quick kick, have one of your midfielders rush to the ball and stand with one foot on it. He can also stand right in front of the ball, preventing the opponent from kicking it forward. If the referee tells the midfielder to move ten yards away, he should get back. Otherwise, the referee might issue him a yellow card for obstruction.

When Mayer steps into the goal at the start of a game, he plays with the same intense concentration in the first minute of the game that he does in the nintieth minute. "I approach every minute and all parts of the game the same way," he said. "Go out there and do the very best you can. Try and stop the opposing players from scoring on you."

Studies have shown that a team has a far better chance of maintaining possession of the ball when it is thrown instead of kicked. Kick the ball when none of your teammates are open to receive it. You can also kick it when you want to waste time or when your opponents are pouring the heat on and you just want to get the ball down to the other end of the field.

It is important for youth goalkeepers to have fun in playing the position. "If you're not having fun, well then you're not enjoying yourself, so you're not performing to your best ability. You have to have the desire to do the best you can to keep the ball out of the back of the net. That takes courage and guts or whatever it takes to play.

"Work as hard as you possibly can because hard work definitely pays off. It's something that I've done all my life. I've worked very hard on my game and I don't take any shortcuts when I play," he explained. "Maybe when practice is over and you don't feel you've had enough, ask some of the players to stay out and take a few more shots on you. It's good for them and good for you."

Phil Parkes
Chicago Sting

Like most successful goalkeepers, Phil Parkes of the Chicago Sting believes that keeping things simple is the best way to play the game.

"I like to play nice and relaxed, just taking things as they come, not playing flashy. I don't see any point diving around for shots when you know yourself that you don't have to," he explained. "I try to make it look as easy as possible."

His consistency and reliability has earned Parkes the NASL's top goalkeeping award for the second consecutive season, chalking up a 0.095 goal-against average.

Parkes has played goalkeeper since he played on his first team. Born in West Bromwich, England on July 14, 1947, he started playing with a soccer ball at about age five. He started out in goal because he liked the position, and also because he did not have to do as much running as the other players. He played goalkeeper on his school teams all the way through school, only playing on the field one game. After that game, he was happy to return to tending the nets.

"I don't know what it was really that wanted me to be a keeper," Parkes said. "I always have been a keeper. I wouldn't change that. If I could do it all over again, I'd still want to be a keeper."

His father often took him to games where he watched how the goalkeeper played his position. Like many English schoolboys, he dreamed of becoming a professional soccer player. He played and practiced whenever he could.

At age 15 he left school and became an apprentice professional on first division West Bromwich's youth team. When he became dissatisfied with the club, he went over to Wolverhampton, another first division club.

In 1964 at age 17 he signed a professional contract with Wolverhampton which was his most memorable youth experience. He enjoyed playing with Wolverhampton for 14 years. During the 1967 offseason, he traveled to Southern California and played for the NASL Los Angeles Wolves.

Parkes did not return to North America until 1976 when Wolverhampton loaned him to Vancouver during the English offseason. His goals-against average with the Whitecaps that year was 1.25. As soon as the NASL season ended, he returned to England and tended the nets for Wolverhampton until 1978 when the Whitecaps purchased his contract. In early 1980, he joined the Chicago Sting.

With a goals-against average of 0.95 for the 1978 season, he earned the title of leading goalkeeper in the NASL. He also had 10 shutouts for the season, games in which no one scored a goal against him.

Of all the coaches he has had since he started playing soccer, he credits Whitecap coach Tony Waiters with having the most beneficial influence on his goalkeeping ability and success in goal.

"All the coaches I have had have helped my career some, but I would say the biggest influence on my career has been Tony Waiters. He was an international goalkeeper himself and the experience means a lot."

One of the hardest tasks of goalkeeping is maintaining concentration the entire 90 minutes of the game. If the ball stays down at the other end of the field, you must prevent your mind from wandering or becoming distracted by the fans.

"Concentration comes with experience. The more experience you get, the better you become at keeping your concentration during the game. There's no substitute for experience really," Parkes said.

He maintains his concentration by watching the ball and by communicating with his defenders. "I like to talk all the

Phil Parkes

while when I am playing. I never stop talking, even when the ball is at the other end. If you're talking with your defenders, that helps you keep your concentration, keep your mind on the game," he noted.

During the game, he tells his defenders where the ball is going to go. When the ball is played in his third of the field, he tells the defenders when they can hold it, if they are free or a forward is trying to tackle, and when to clear the ball forward as fast as possible.

"It is important that the goalkeeper talks because he sees everything going on," Parkes said. "Since he is the one that is beyond everybody, he can see things like a play developing on the left side that a right fullback can't see or a winger trying to get behind a defender for a pass or take the ball off him."

When your team is on the attack and the other team gains possession of the ball, shout to your forwards and midfielders to mark an opponent and get the ball back. Shout encouragement to them and your defenders all through the game.

When the ball is in the opponents' half of the field, come out six to eight yards. If an opponent gains possession of the ball and chips it over your defenders' head for an opposing forward to run onto, you may be able to sprint forward and get the ball without endangering your own goal. Only come out for a through pass, if you are sure that you can get the ball before an opponent.

"The farther the ball is back, the farther you would be out. If the ball is in their half of the field, you would be out somewhere around the penalty spot. The closer it comes in, the farther you drop back toward your own goal line," Parkes explained. "You don't want it chipped over your head into the goal before you can get back and catch it."

If an unmarked opponent dribbles the ball into the penalty area you have to start coming out and narrowing your angle. If at least one of your defenders is on him, you would stay back and wait to see if the opponent beat your defense. If he managed to get past your defenders, then you will have to come out and meet him, according to Parkes.

"If a forward breaks through, don't commit yourself too early. If you can take the ball off his feet, come out and dive at his feet," he said. "If you don't get that chance, just try to make yourself as big as possible. If you dive too early, he can go the other way and shoot.

"You've got to make him do what you want him to do. If the fellow has broken through and has the ball under control, you've got to come out slowly, approach him slowly. If you rush him, he's just going to dribble around you and put it in the back of the net. So you've got to come out, jockey him, try and make him knock it past you. Keep yourself in a position where he can't chip it over your head. Always put yourself between the ball and the goal."

When you come out after the forward with the ball, always put your weight on your toes. Crouch a little bit with your knees slightly bent for better balance. You need proper balance to move in whatever direction your opponent pushes the ball. If you lose your balance, he will push the ball past you and score. Avoid being tense and nervous. Try to be as relaxed as possible.

Forget trying to guess which way the forward will go with the ball or what is going on in his mind. If you anticipate that he plans to go left and you move before he does, he will push the ball to the right, catch you off balance, dribble past you and score.

"If you try and anticipate what the forward is going to do, you'll get beat more times than if you stay on your feet," Parkes said. "Don't commit yourself, force the forward to commit himself. Then the minute you think that you can get the ball, dive at his feet and get it."

If you keep your eye on the ball instead of the forward's feet, you will not fall for any of his fakes, no matter how he dances around the ball and tries to get you off-balance. If you look away from the ball, even for a second, that will be the time he tries to make his move past you.

"When you go after the ball, dive with your arms and head first. Don't worry about getting injured. If you start worrying about getting injured, it's time to pack it in," Parkes said. "Concentrate on the ball and know that you're going to get it. The more experience you have, the more confidence you will have."

When a forward takes a power shot from the 18-yard line

or farther out, you can expect the ball will hit with a lot of speed and force. Watch the ball and get your body behind it. Catch the ball with your hands behind it. If you try to catch it with your hands down the sides, the ball may go through your hands and bounce off your chest. If you cannot catch the ball, then punch it wide.

During training sessions, Parkes spends most of his time on sharp reaction drills. "We never do a lot of shooting from way out on the edge of the box. It's all close in," he said. "You're talking shooting from 8-10 yards and sometimes closer than that. It's all very quick reactions. We run through 10-15 minutes and then change over."

One typical drill calls for a shooter to have several balls about seven or eight yards out from goal. When he pushes a ball towards the corner of the goal, you are forced to dive, save it, and throw it back. Then the shooter pushes the ball into another corner, forcing you to dive in the opposite direction.

In another drill, place a cone about eight to ten yards straight out in front of each goalpost. Then have a forward dribble up to the cone, go around wide of the cone, and take a shot on goal. To widen the angle, you can place the cones on the edge of the six-yard box.

"You wouldn't be standing on your line when they come in, you'd be trying to cut the angles down," Parkes said. "If you have them shooting from angles, you can add a forward to come in for any ball that rebounds off you like."

In an offense-defense drill, you put the defenders on the goalposts and forwards in the middle of the goal. The coach stands just to one side of the goal and throws in a ball. The defenders have to get out and block it before the forwards can shoot. If a forward gets his foot on the ball, the goalkeeper has to save it.

Also work on crosses and throwing at the same time. When the ball is crossed from the right wing and you catch it, throw it immediately to an open player on the left wing. This requires that you are always aware of where everyone is on the field, even during attacks on your goal. If you know where your open teammates are on the left wing when you catch a ball crossed from the right wing, you gain both time and open space for your team when you immediately throw the ball to a teammate on the left.

"Most of our practices are done in game situations. When there is nobody there to challenge you, you tend to get into faults," he said. "Small sided games are the best."

Parks did a lot of agility training early in his career, exercises like rolling the ball back through his legs, turning around, and chasing it. For conditioning now, he does about 200 sit-ups everyday.

At age 32 Parks is just entering his prime goalkeeping years. While most field players retire from professional soccer in their early thirties, goalkeepers do not tend to amass all the skills and experience they need to become a top keeper until they go beyond thirty years of age. Some professional goalkeepers play well into their forties.

Experience is important in defending against a cross or corner kick. Have your defenders try to keep their opponents as far away from the goal line as possible. The more room you have in front of the goal to catch the ball, the better your chances of making the save. Always make sure that every opponent in front of the goal is marked. If an opposing forward is unmarked, he can be very dangerous.

In corner-kick situations, make sure every opponent is marked. Then position a teammate on the near post as well as on the far post. Their responsibility is to be sure no opponent gets behind you and also to clear the ball off the line. Also position a teammate on the edge of the six-yard area level with the near post. If the opponent taking the corner kick drives the ball in low and hard, your teammate has to cut the shot off and get the ball forward.

"Watch the ball. You should be about in the center of the goal, a yard or so off your line. Just watch the ball. You can't make your move until the ball is kicked," he advised. "You have to move towards the ball. When you come out, shout to your defenders. They've got to get out of the way so you can get up there and get the ball. You will know from instinct whether you can catch or if you'll have to punch it out. If you punch it, hit it as far and wide as you can."

Concentrate on the ball. Avoid thinking about any opponents in your way. If you worry about your opponents, you cannot concentrate on the ball. Bring your knee up for protection when you go up for a ball. Forget about everything else but getting the ball.

When you catch the ball, throw it to an open teammate on the opposite wing. Throw the ball instead of kicking it because you can throw a ball with far greater accuracy than you can achieve by kicking it. If you kick the ball, the opposing defenders have almost as much chance of winning the ball as your teammates. The only time you kick the ball is when there is no one open or when you want to slow the game down.

"I'm reluctant to throw balls down the middle," he said. "I tend to throw balls wide rather than down the middle. Balls thrown down the middle are typically balls midfielders can get, but somebody can close them down quickly, and you want to avoid that."

If a winger is open for a pass, throw the ball to him because he is the farthest forward. If the winger is marked tight, throw the ball to the midfielder, if he is out wide to the touchline and in open space. If the midfielders and wingers are marked tight, throw the ball to an open fullback. If no one is open, kick it to the forward who is the most open. Everything depends on the situation.

When you throw, try to place the ball at your teammate's feet or in open space he can run onto. Practice your throwing until you can throw a ball to the halfway line with pinpoint accuracy.

"In soccer every situation is different. Get as much experience as you can," Parkes explained. "Work as hard as you can. Being a soccer player is hard work. A lot of people think it's easy because you play for an hour-and-a-half and train for two to three hours a day. We do more in those two to three hours than most people do in a day's work. To get something out of the game, you've got to work really hard. You get out of it what you put into it."

Bob Rigby
Philadelphia Fury

An outstanding athlete with physical strength and jumping ability, goalkeeper Bob Rigby has earned 25 shutouts in seven seasons in the North American Soccer League. He still holds the record for the lowest goals-against average in a season with 0.62 set in 1973. As an NASL veteran, Rigby gained a reputation as someone who is tough to beat.

Born in Ridley Park, Pennsylvania on July 3, 1951, Rigby, like most of today's American professionals, got a late start on his soccer career. He did not start playing until he was in sixth grade when youth soccer organizations were few and far between.

"The local high school and junior high school coaches thought it would be a good idea if they would get kids into soccer before they went to junior high school. In the spring they ran a big soccer clinic and played games with all the different elementary schools that fed the junior and senior high schools. It was a big tournament with all the elementary schools against each other so we played all spring."

Although many of his classmates played soccer in junior high school, Rigby played football from the seventh through the ninth grade. In grammar school and junior high, he played baseball and some basketball.

"I finally started playing soccer on the team in the tenth

grade because it was more fun. I hadn't really enjoyed football," Rigby recalled. "When I went to high school, football was the end all, be all. I think a lot of kids would have loved to play soccer, but the thing to do was to play football. I just got to the point where I wanted enjoyment out of playing a sport so I played soccer."

Instead of playing goalkeeper, he played in the midfield and in the defense. After the high school soccer season ended, he played all through the winter on a team in the United League, a junior youth soccer league in the Philadelphia area.

His high school soccer team went to the state semi-finals in his junior year and had good prospects for a better season the following year. Then the team's goalkeeper moved at the end of Rigby's junior year, leaving a doubtful question mark about the team's chances for the state championship the next season so Rigby was asked to step in.

"I think I owe a lot to my high school coach Jack Preston. If he had not gotten me into goal, I don't think I would have made the transition by myself. He convinced me that I could do well at it," Rigby said. "When I knew that I was going to have to play in goal, I spent a lot of time during the summer between my junior and senior year working with him. He had a good bunch of people around me that would show almost every night, everybody really took a lot of time and worked hard. That helped me a lot."

The team did not win the state championship, but he had 11 shutouts for the season.

After high school, he played four years in goal on the varsity team for East Stroudsburg State College in Pennsylvania. He was twice named All-American, 1972 and 1973, and was selected to play in the first Senior Bowl. During the college off-seasons, he played in the United League.

His college coach Dr. John McKeon helped him broaden his game experience. In his freshman year, McKeon took him to the Olympic trials in Baltimore, but he lost out to an older goalkeeper with more experience.

"He gave me many opportunities to get around and play against foreign teams that were touring here. So he really helped my development by getting me a lot more exposure

Bob Rigby

than I could have gotten for myself. He was really instrumental in developing me," he said. After his senior year, he spent part of the summer in Europe.

Rigby was the No. 1 draft choice after college graduation in 1973. He was selected by the Philadelphia Atoms which held the Philadelphia NASL franchise at that time. Coached by Al Miller, he and his teammates won the NASL Championship that year. He was then selected for the U.S. National Team and played under the famous coach Dettmar Cramer.

Rigby played two more seasons for the Atoms before being traded to the New York Cosmos for the 1976 season. After tending goal for 15 games, he broke his collarbone and was out the rest of the season. Then the Los Angeles Aztecs purchased his contract for the following season where he played until halfway through the 1979 season when the Fury brought him to Philadelphia.

Pregame mental preparation is most important to goalkeepers as well as field players, according to Rigby.

"A couple of hours before the game, I like to think a bit about my game, and if there is anything that is unique about the other team, such as they have a big center forward who they like to pass to or a good winger that gets around in back," Rigby explained. "Basically as a goalkeeper you want to just think about the things that you're going to do in the game. The easiest thing to do as a goalkeeper is you want to play the same way against every team.

"It's also important you recognize the strong points in your game and your own weaknesses, and the way you want to play. You have to sit back and concentrate a little bit on what you're going to have to do in specific situations. Try to envision yourself playing the game and doing everything as it comes naturally. There's a lot of thought behind it. You have to do this hundreds and hundreds of times as you grow as a player to the point it does become automatic," he said.

"Know your opponents' strengths and weaknesses as well, but don't worry about any particular players. Respect is one thing, fear is another," he said. "You can't worry more about the person than the ball. You can never lose concentration. A player's reputation gets around, kick this guy, or you look crossed eyed at him and he gets all upset and he forgets about the game a little bit. Then people are going to try and upset you. You can't let this happen."

The better you concentrate on the game, the better your self-confidence. "You need to feel that you can handle any situation with any given player. It's important not only from the standpoint of having confidence in yourself, but also from the team standpoint. You can exude confidence through the whole team, or you can have a detrimental effect on the team," Rigby said. "Goalkeeping is a position where you want a calm person back there. If a teammate looks at you and says to himself, 'If he doesn't look worried, why should I be worried', then you have given him some self-confidence.

I think that is important. It's best just to try to keep your emotions in and concentrate on your goalkeeping."

If your teammates are fighting up front, trying to score a goal, and you allow a goal scored against you because of carelessness or a clumsy mistake, this has a demoralizing effect on the team. Always be on your toes and give 100 percent every second of the game. The better you play your game in goal, the more confidence everyone on the field will have in the team.

Avoid being flashy, Rigby says. Do not dive for a ball that you can take standing up. While some fans might enjoy watching you dive around, the people who really understand soccer know that the goalkeeper who stays on his feet is superior to somebody throwing himself around the goal. Once you dive, you are on the ground, and unable to spring immediately back into position. If you dive and punch a ball back out into the field, you may not be able to get up in time to stop the next shot. If you stay on your feet, you are ready for anything that happens.

"The goalkeeper is in a position where he can really ham it up, if he wants to," Rigby said. "This is what over the years weeds out the good from the bad. There are hundreds of people who can fly around and make the action saves, and do one or two great things. It's the people who play consistent games year after year that make it. They don't let any stupid goals get in the back of the net. Maybe a great shot beats them, maybe it doesn't sometimes. You have to do the thing that is the safest, which is a very important part of goalkeeping. Try and not look too flashy."

Many goals are scored not because of the attackers' brilliance, but because of a mistake committed in the defense. If a defender tries to clear a ball and misplays it in front of the goal, your concentration must be so high that you instinctly are ready for the mistake and can get the ball before an opposing forward can put it in the back of the net. If a defender takes on a forward with the ball in a one-on-one situation in front of the goal, and moves too much to the right giving the forward a shot on goal, you must tell your defender to move left and properly position yourself at the same time. Since there are so many different situations in which mistakes can occur, you cannot learn to handle them all through drills and exercises.

"I think it's just a matter of experience over the years. The more times you run across those situations, the better you'll be able to react a little more quickly. It's just a matter of getting as many games under your belt as you can, and hopefully, you will be able to realize some of the things you've had trouble with. It's a matter of reading the game, reading the situation and the outcome of the situation," he observed. "Experience is really the end-all, be-all for the goalkeeper. The game becomes easy for you after you've played enough games."

Narrowing the angle is one of the most important techniques that every goalkeeper must learn. "The best goalkeepers are the guys who always make everything look fairly simple, and have great positional sense. All your positioning is done in relation to where the ball is on the field and your near post, the goalpost closest to the ball, he said. "You just go out far enough so that you can get back to your near post, if you have to. One of the cardinal sins in goalkeeping is getting scored on your near post. So you always position yourself instinctively with that in mind."

How you come out from the goal is also vitally important. If you stand on your goal line, you have not narrowed the angle. If you go out too far, the forward will have a better chance of dribbling around you and taking a shot. A lot depends on the individual, especially height. A tall goalkeeper can afford to stay closer to the goal than a shorter player because the taller goalkeeper can spread his arms out and protect more area than a shorter goalkeeper. When you come out you also have to know how fast you can get back for those times a forward tries to chip a ball over your head.

"There is no one spot that is right for every goalkeeper. Everyone is stronger on one side or the other, and some guys have got more range than others," Rigby said. "So every individual goalkeeper has to find out on his own what is best for him and how he wants to play it."

Some goalkeepers are very quick coming off their line and like to play one-on-one with the opposing forward with the ball. Other goalkeepers who may not be as quick are shot stoppers and position themselves well. They prefer to have the forward come in and shoot before he gets too close to him. Every goalkeeper can develop his own individual style of play which is best suited for him.

Learn to use your defenders' positioning to your advantage. "If a defender goes after the forward attacking the goal, the defender is going to push him one way or the other. If the defender goes in from the left, the guy is probably going to have to escape to the right to get away," he said. "This helps you as a goaltender in anticipating what will happen next."

You can try to fake the shooter sometimes by giving him a little more space on one side or the other. Fake to the left by leaning a little to the left, and then throw yourself to the right. When the shooter sees you lean left, he thinks you have opened up a scoring opportunity on the right, and shoots. This is why you must go to the right as soon as you have faked to the left. If you fail to get back, he will shoot the ball past you into the back of the net.

Forwards often try to fake goalkeepers in one-on-one situations. "They use body feints, dummy the ball, pretend they're going to shoot, and then they don't, or fake to get you off balance," Rigby said. "There is not any set way of spotting the fake. Be patient and watch the ball. Wait for whatever is going to happen happen. You don't go off the handle yourself. That is something that just comes with experience."

When a forward comes at you with the ball and puts his head down to look at the ball, you know he is getting ready to strike the ball. If he leans back, the shot will be high. If he is over the top of the ball, his shot will stay low. If he hits the ball with the inside of his foot, he is going to try and place the ball. If he strikes the ball with his shoelaces, he wants to drive it with a power shot.

Watch various forwards and observe their styles of attack. "Learn everything you can" Rigby said. "I would like to stress to everybody to have a really open mind. Be able to take coaching and criticism because there's a lot of improvement that everyone, including me, can still make in his game. Be receptive and try and learn as fast as you can. Try to become a student of the game yourself. Just don't depend on coaching. Sift out the good advice from the bad, but be humble about it and have an open mind becuse there is always something to learn that can help you no matter if you're a player six-years-old or 60."